GUIDELINES FOR PREPARING THE RESEARCH PROPOSAL

Revised Edition

John H. Behling, Ph.D.

College of Social Work
The Ohio State University
Columbus, Ohio

UNIVERSITY
PRESS OF
AMERICA

LANHAM • NEW YORK • LONDON

Copyright © 1984 by

University Press of America,™ Inc.

4720 Boston Way
Lanham. MD 20706

3 Henrietta Street
London WC2E 8LU England

Library of Congress Cataloging in Publication Data

Behling, John H.
  Guidelines for preparing the research proposal.

  Bibliography: p.
  1. Social sciences—Research—Methodology. 2. Social
service—Research—Methodology. 3. Proposal writing in
the social sciences—Methodology. I. Title.
H62.B3634   1984   808'.066361   83-23362
ISBN 0-8191-3733-2 (alk. paper)
ISBN 0-8191-3734-0 (pbk. : alk. paper)

PREFACE

The purpose of this monograph is to facilitate the process of preparing research ideas for presentation to those groups, authorities and sponsors that give necessary support for the successful study and investigation of problems in the human service and social science areas. Hopefully, this monograph will reduce the loss of investigation into significant problem areas because of inadequate presentation of the research proposal document.

These materials are organized around three principle areas of interest to researchers: first, an introduction to the problem to be studied; second, a review of literature relevant to the problem and third, a methodological statement as to how to carry out the investigation of the problem.

The scope of these materials will not include the subtle devices of "grantsmanship" because any worthy project well prepared and presented will include the basic components of "grantsmanship." That is to say, the intent of this material on the preparation and presentation of research proposals is not to help the proposal writer outwit the sponsors or grantors as the term "grantsmanship" implies. Rather, it is hoped that grantors are concerned with funding projects that serve to build knowledge and contribute useful information to the solution of problems large and small in scope. However, Part V is devoted to a few basic principles of grantsmanship for the beginner.

Many readers may feel that the materials presented here tend to emphasize survey and experimental designs more than historical and qualitative case study designs. To a great extent this reflects the bias of the organization forms and outlines which the various agencies require. But primary emphasis reflects the bias of college and university departments or private human service organizations. Supplementary suggestions are made throughout these materials to aid proposal writers in regard to other kinds of studies and designs.

John H. Behling
October, 1983

TABLE OF CONTENTS

NOTES BEFORE BEGINNING THE PROPOSAL

WHY WRITE A RESEARCH PROPOSAL?

It is quite unnecessary to answer the question "Why write a research proposal?" if the question is addressed to professional researchers, evaluators, and grant proposal writers. To such persons the reasons are obvious and go without mention. However, for those who are students in academic programs requiring thesis or dissertation research, the question takes on serious meaning. It is equally true for professional educators, social workers, city planners and staff members of small social, civic and community organizations who have little experience with "getting money" or "grantsmanship" for projects of service and research. The following arguments should be sufficient to convince most who are serious about carrying out a research project.

The research proposal is a necessary document to convince funding sources, sponsors, and academic bodies that the project is worthy of their attention let alone their money. In the case of academic institutions the research proposal is essential to convince the appropriate committees of the value of the project as it may contribute to a body of knowledge. This would seem to be a sufficient reason to prepare a proposal, but there are other equally compelling reasons for preparing a proposal.

The proposal is a study plan that is to be followed in the course of the research effort. It should be thought of as a device to be used as a guide in the development of the research process. To the extent that the proposal is a plan it establishes an order to one's research effort. It gives a continuity to the various steps and stages of the work to be done.

The proposal helps the researcher to organize his efforts in terms of time to be spent and resources to commit to the project. After all, a project may sound and seem reasonable enough to do except when it is worked out in detail and one discovers that the time or expenses are beyond one's resources. The proposal forces one to consider these two issues.

Not only are time and resource important, but so is general feasibility. If one needs to learn a new language in order to carry out a project, it would seem better if another aspect of the topic would be explored. If one had to acquire specialized training in order to carry out a project, its feasibility would appear in doubt. If an extremely controversial topic is being considered as a research project, unrelated issues may so entangle the research effort that its feasibility would, again, appear in doubt.

The process of writing a proposal actually forces the author to think through various steps of the research process. That is, the proposal writing process forces a direction of thought that shapes the project and the procedures for carrying it out. To put it another way, the proposal preparation process is a thinking-through process.

In more formal terms the proposal is a series of statements which are designed to carry forward an action for the purpose of testing a specific set of hypotheses. The proposal serves as a guide to the hypothesis testing process which embodies the specific purpose of the study effort.

Finally, the research proposal as written following the outline described in Part II or any other outline model for that matter, serves as the basis for the writing of the first three chapters of the final research report. The final report will logically include an Introduction, Review of Literature and a Methodology. The proposal once written and used can easily be converted to chapters in the research report.

GENERATING IDEAS

When a proposal is in the process of being prepared, it is obvious that a topic has been selected and its refinement is well under way. However, many researchers, grant writers and especially students may be looking for ideas that will eventually lead to the preparation of a research proposal. More often than not, the writer has an idea, but it lacks substance, clarity, conceptualization, and everything else that makes it more than an idea. There are plenty of ideas floating around that are in this stage. The quality of these ideas is terribly important and should not be overlooked as a factor of value in the research process and will be dealt with shortly. At this point how does one move an idea from its simplicity as a thought to a set of workable concepts within a theoretical framework?

Begin by writing down thoughts about your idea. Note-taking is and should be a highly regarded scientific activity. Note-taking is a means of playing with thoughts and fragments of ideas. It is a process by which one fits together ideas and pieces of ideas as if one were working out a jig saw puzzle. The note-taking stage should take on the dimensions of an obsession. The writing of notes should be, at this stage, impulsive and obsessive. Don't worry about the randomness of this process, for in time a pattern will begin to form and the bits and pieces will fall into place. Don't rush the note-taking process for it is an idea-hunting method and takes time.

Talk to as many people as you can who are knowledgeable in the area of you idea. Such persons will frequently lead you to new or additional material. Such persons are frequently very willing to spend time with you, but others will be much less willing to give of their time and this posture should be respected. Experts or specialists are busy with their own work. Yet, there are those who are kind enough to discuss their ideas wtih you. In this regard, do not limit yourself to experts. Discuss your idea with anyone who is willing to listen. This writer has found some of the most valuable ideas expressed by non-expert persons.

Read widely. It goes without saying that you must read a great deal before you can be satisfied that your idea is shared by others. Other writers have developed material in your idea area and can contribute to yours. Continue to do the general reading that you are normally inclined to consume, for your idea has a way of popping up in the oddest places. Actually you are, at this stage, in the process of holding your idea close to the front of your mind and any material that passes before you is automatically perused for its relatedness to the idea. This is why it is equally important not to limit yourself to the pedantic journals because ideas are found everywhere if your radar, so to speak, is turned on. There are many, many popular or mass consumption journals, newspapers and magazines that may very well add useful facets and information to your idea. The presentation of information is not neatly organized by the literary world into important and non-important scientific material. This is especially true of original and futuristic ideas. Very often science-fiction and artistic presentations express the newest ideas. Again, my suggestion is to read widely and talk to a diverse group of people to give needed substance to your idea.

In the development of your idea, be sure to allow for a substantial lapse of time from its origination to the time when you start writing your research proposal. It is important not to hurry this development because it needs time to mature or wither. It is very possible that the idea will lose its fascination or substance. It is possible that others will have covered the idea so thoroughly that your own interest is weakened and perhaps lost. But more importantly you must have the time to examine the nuances of all the material that is added to your idea. Actually, as your idea formulates and takes creditable shape, the maturing will have occurred. At this point you will have moved from informal idea hunting toward a more formal review of literature which will be discussed in Part III.

DON'T BE AFRAID TO BE CREATIVE

The problems that confront us as professionals and non-professionals seem endless in number. Many of these problems, perhaps most, are a consequence of higher expectations for one's life. The more we expect, the more complexities and dissatisfactions are encountered. The solutions to these problems are difficult to come by as multifaceted complexities inundate the problem situation. Frequently, researchers will build their research plans on the shoulders of previous research efforts. This approach is traditional and very sound scientifically speaking. It is a building block procedure that starts with a foundation of well validated knowledge. All of this is well and good but it does not explain nor account for the failure to produce effective solutions in the case of many problems. It does not account for the serendipitous solution to a problem, nor does it account for inadvertent discoveries as a result of accidents and unintentional miscues in procedure. Careful searching of the literature is an absolute necessity in the preparation of any study and solution to problems. What needs to be emphasized here is a few words of encouragement for proposal writers to be more creative in approaching a problem.

As you look for material, do not limit yourself to other people's ideas. Nor should you limit yourself by thinking you must accept the totality of someone else's idea or thoery. You can extract any part of an idea or theory and build on it with your own thinking. Remember, your own ideas have just as much potential as the next fellow's, and maybe more. Don't rely on the most authoritative person in a field. You should certainly study their writings and their research but your own creativity may equal and possibly surpass even the most imposing of authorities. Don't be afraid to dismantle someone else's theory and take that which best fits your conceptualization. Everyone has had the experience, upon hearing about a

4

new idea, of saying "I thought of that a long time ago." Most everyone has had ideas that were criticized for being too ridiculous, too far out, only to discover with the passage of time that someone else has developed the same idea and accumulated fame and fortune in the process. Not all of our ideas have achieved such dramatic ends, but the point that ideas have validity without formal institutional backing is true for most of us.

The real limit to whatever ingenious notions and ideas we may develop is our own imagination. We need to stretch our thinking in order to develop new possibilities. In the process of studying and pondering literature in a particular area of interest, the logic of the author is always subject to interpretation. Why didn't the author consider a different line of thinking? Inquiry is a serious matter and should be done boldly, whether applied to innovation or ponderous theoretical matter. Critical assessment of long held beliefs is the first step to new interpretation of historical events and other so called scientific truths. The knowledgeable authorities occupy the institutional front row only because others have abandoned the effort. The promoters of solar energy have long been considered slightly less than ridiculous for thinking that this kind of energy could be economically produced. We now know that solar energy is an idea whose time has come. Any and all ideas about alternative sources of energy are seriously being considered and explored. The creative spirit still lives. Don't be afraid to exercise it even within the pedantic halls of higher learning.

WRITING STYLE

Writing a research proposal is an exercise in providing detail that will answer the questions of any reader or reviewer. Normally there should be a good deal of detail that satisfies the expert or reviewer, and yet not so much detail that the person unfamiliar with the topic gets lost in a maze of discussion. The right balance of detail should help the reader quickly grasp the nature of the problem and your approach to it. The best advice is to write close to your proposal outline (at least the first draft). Write clearly and simply. But some detail is always needed unless you are writing a one or two page abstract. Good proposal writing is a delicate balance of presenting your intentions in dealing with your research problem. You should describe the research in enough detail that the sponsor or reviewer is satisfied that the problem is worth investigation and that the researcher has the capacity to carry it out to a satisfactory conclusion. It should be remembered that it is impossible to anticipate every minor detail, and this is well understood by sponsors, advisors, and reviewers.

When writing even the first draft of your proposal, take care to see that there is a logical flow from one section to another . After all, the proposal, like the research that flows from it, is like a chain of reasoning that moves smoothly from one concern to another without confusing interruptions. One good example of this flow is implicit in the Introduction section of the research proposal outline. The "area of concern" is followed by "problem statement," followed by "purpose," followed by "major research question," followed by "minor research questions" and so on. This sequence of topics begins with a very general statement and continue to narrow down to very specific detailed material. A good proposal will reflect this kind of reasoning with each section reflecting the previous section and carrying it one step further in a consistent manner. Too often the beginning writer of proposals will complain of this apparent overlapping and see it as duplication.

The proposal is a chain of logic built carefully and slowly so that after the final page is read, a clear, complete picture will be comprehended by the reiveweer.

When doubt is raised in your mind regarding your material, it is best to stop and re-write that portion. It is good practice to write your proposal word for word as if it were the final draft. Obviously, at this point you are working from an outline as well as notes so that the final draft feeling is with you as you strive for the final draft look of your proposal.

How can others help you in writing your proposal? Always have others read over your material in order to identify gaps, flaws and oversights of various kinds. Weaknesses in organization and writing style are frequently most easily detected either by those unfamiliar with the proposal or by the writer himself after a span of time has elapsed and thereby giving the writer a different perspective. Even the most skillful proposal writer can benefit from a critical reading by a second party. More often than not a reader unfamiliar with your work will give you some of the most helpful suggestions.

One of the most common failures on the part of first time proposal writers is lack of clarity regaring the central purpose of the endeavor. Very often first time writers will overlook the obvious in favor of the esoteric and complex. In regard to complexity, it is most important to define in text writing uncommon terms in an honest effort to communicate. Some authors write obscurely for reasons of ego building and self-reassurance of the proposal's importance. Write clearly and write simply.

Good writing, especially research proposal writing, should involve the use of punctuation, spacing, underlining, drawing, charts, tables, frequent use of subheadings in order to attract your reader's full attention. When possible list items in order of importance or in terms of logical sequence. This is a part of outlining which gives order and structure to your work. After all, this is not poetry or the great American novel you are writing.

FORMAT

David Krathwohl (1966) in his manual, "How to Prepare a Research Proposal" deals with format and proposal appearance in the following way:

> How important is the appearance of the proposal? Some institutions'
> research offices do a very careful and complete job of preparing the
> proposal in attractive form. Their proposals arrive in spiral bindings
> with printed covers and multilithed text. One cannot say that the
> reader will be unimpressed by this, but certainly it is unessential. In
> some instances the spiral bindings and cover are removed in order to
> more easily send the material through the mails to the readers.
> Simple dittoed proposals have and will continue to be approved.
> Certainly the major effort should be on legibility, readability, and
> clarity of presentation. (p. 23)

The reader must remember that Krathwohl is addressing himself to grant proposal writing more than he is academic proposals such as theses and dissertations. Nevertheless, there are a number of additional points to be made in favor of careful consideration of format and the physical layout of the proposal.

Fortunately or unfortunately there is an impressive message hidden in the physical presences of any kind of material. Marshall McLuhan has popularized the phrase, "The Medium is the Message" (McLuhan, 1967) to which I enthusiastically agree. Students are always discounting the physical appearance of their work claiming that the ideas or content of the work is what is important to focus on. The appearance or "presence" of material is far more dominant than the ideas spelled out as content. McLuhan claims that the very fact that the medium is discounted makes it all the more dominant and instructive. It is "telling" you things well before the content is examined. For example, the elaborate care taken to prepare and present material tells the reader much about the commitment the author has to the ideas and material presented. That is, if an author cares enough to laboriously and meticulously present his ideas, then he surely considers the ideas to be worthy of such effort. In summary, the physical apearance is very important; even though it will not sell poorly conceived ideas, it goes a long way toward selling well conceived ideas.

The length of a research proposal is always an issue that must be dealt with during the writing of any material. Frequently, sponsors, government agencies, foundations and academic advisors spell out in very specific terms the necessary length of documents such as research requests and proposals. This presents no problem. That kind of instruction is simply followed; otherwise it is best to include information you feel important to the reader rather than omit it. If the writer feels strongly about including drawings, citations, and explanations, then by all means include such material.

Don't crowd text material into sections that would read better if such materials were placed in an appendix (at the end of your work) to the proposal. This allows the reader to deal with as much material as he may wish, reading appendix material or not. Try to avoid forcing your reviewer to read through voluminous material of questionable value to him.

Underlining material and especially important phrases and key words breaks up page after page of copy and places emphasis where you wish your reader to focus close attention.

Always use good quality paper, especially for the final draft. Be generous with the use of this paper and avoid crowding at the bottom of a page in an effort to save paper. Even the best quality paper is cheap by comparison to the value of your ideas.

Always make several copies of your final draft for it is important that extra copies are always in your possession. Frequently strange things will happen to your original draft. Remember others may find your work sufficiently interesting to borrow a copy. When a first or second draft is being loaned to a friend for his or her critical assessment, it is important to make extra copies.

Have the final draft placed in a plastic binder with a handsomely designed cover. Here again at least two copies should be prepared. There are plenty of commercial printers that enjoy doing this kind of thing for a small price.

There may well be drawings, charts, tables, maps, photographs and pictures used in your proposal. Great care should be taken to make sure that these kinds of graphic presentations are not crowded or otherwise made unattractive. These kinds of graphic arts add a great deal to the communication of your ideas; therefore, care should be taken to maximize their positive effect.

Leave wide margins on both sides of each page. This provides the reader or reviewer ample opportunity to write notes in regard to your material. It also provides you the same opportunity if revisions are necessary.

Use a new typewriter ribbon for your final draft. Of course, if a professional typist does your work, and that is strongly advised, it will be returned typed in heavy dark print type (Turabian, 1955).

Finally, it is important to number all pages beginning with the Introductory page as number one and continuing until the final page is attached. They should be numbered on all drafts in order that revisions will be easily referred to in the writing process.

ORGANIZATION AND PLANNING FOR THE PROPOSAL WRITING TASKS

The secret to writing a high quality research proposal is good organization. Good clear organization will make your points in telling fashion because it is organization of the proposal that quickly carries the reader through your material. From such a reading the points are clear and their connectedness obvious. The key to organization is the development of an outline. You may design your own outline or follow the suggested outline detailed in Part II. Part II presents the outline and Part III explains how each section and topic may be handled.

In the actual preparation for the writing task it is most important to allow yourself fairly large blocks of time such as two to four hours of uninterrupted time. It is most wise to locate yourself where there will be no interruptions so that your concentration will be intense and sharp. It is difficult to do any serious writing other than office memos when there are frequent interruptions to one's line of thought. YOu must get away from people including the tools of communication--the telephone.

You should have all your materials at hand and most especially your notes, references, articles and writing materials. Your reference materials should be sorted out and grouped together around each subheading within the proposal outline.

Once all arrangements are made, the final step in getting ready is the setting of target dates for finishing various phases of the proposal writing task. Above all, stick to your writing or work schedule (at all costs). Progress achieved in this way will in turn increase your motivation for accomplishing a high quality end product.

Many writers will be familiar with these suggestions but many first time proposal writers will need all the help they can get.

UNDERSTANDING THE RESEARCH PROCESS

Before undertaking the task of writing a research proposal, it is assumed that some knowledge of research methodology is understood by the writer. It is quite possible that one can write proposals for grants centered on the rendering of some service or program. For example, a training program for public welfare workers could be the object of a special grant. A proposal written to justify such a grant would not be a research proposal although it would more than likely include a section on how the training program might be evaluated. There are many such proposals being written and they do not require any special training or skill in the area of research methodology. However, if the researcher had such skills it would be very helpful to the writing process. Remember these guidelines are not designed to help individuals with such intentions. If the writer is not skilled in research methodology, it is highly recommended that an elementary course in the subject be taken before or at least during the writing of the proposal. The only other alternative is to employ someone who has the skill of a trained methodologist to at least guide your hand in drafting the very technical parts of the outline discussed in Part II.

Before beginning the proposal writing task, an overall understanding of the research process is essential to the writer. The research process is made up of a number of closely related steps that frequently overlap rather than following a strictly outlined series of sequential steps (Selltiz, et al., 1959: 8-9). The emphasis is on the work "process" where activity is moving along on several different phases of the overall project. When the instruments of data collection are being planned, sampling procedures are being considerd. If the instruments to be administered require personal interviews, then the researcher must reconsider the size of his sample of respondents. A long personal interview is costly and the researcher's budget may be limited. This kind of thinking and activity is going on during the planning and execution of any project. The point is that the research process is a series of highly related activities that are being done seemingly all at the same time. The research process is quite different from the steps in the scientific method. It differs in that it does not follow a neat linear step by step pattern from problem statement to study design, to data collection to analysis of data, to findings and interpretation of the findings. Nor does the research process look anything like the final research report or published article. The research process involves many activities that will never be reported in the published document. For example, the research proposal outline recommended in Part II will take the writer into problem areas of getting personal interviews and retrieving returns from a mailed questionnaire. Such problems are rarely ever mentioned in the final report. The planning in regard to budget is never mentioned in the scientific method of the final research report. The coding and coding instruction used in preparing the data for computer analysis will not be discussed in the final report. The calendar and timetable carefully planned with deadline dates in the research proposal will not be referred to at all in the final report. The experienced researcher will begin a project by doing several different activities of the research process simultaneously. He will think little of such a beginning whereas it may look like confusion and chaos to the beginner. When you design hypotheses, you plan your data collection instrument, coding, coding instruction, data analysis design, and even comments on the possible results. It is not all that simple; but to the old hand, these activities overlap and develop in a special rhythmic way that is best understood when professional competence is applied to research work.

The research process is embedded in the research proposal outline discussed in Part II. It is hoped that in preparing the proposal using the recommended outline that the beginning proposal writer will gain a clear sense of the research process and the excitement of research enterprise.

RESEARCH PROPOSAL OUTLINE EXPLANATION

ORGANIZATION OF THE PROPOSAL OUTLINE

A skeleton outline of the recommended research proposal is located in the latter part of this section. The outline begins with a title page which the writer will want to examine for various characteristics that will aid the proposal writer in designing and laying out the proper information in an efficient format. A table of contents follows the cover page before the topical areas are presented. As for the main body of the outline, the reader can see it is laid out with major subheadings and minor side subheadings that appear as incomplete sentences with topical headings as starters. Briefly examining the outline one can see that the research proposal outline is divided into three major sections or chapters preceded with a recommended title page and table of contents. The first section is made up of nine basic subheadings and is the "Introduction." The second section is the Review of Literature, and is composed of three major subheadings. The third section is the methodology with the largest number of subheadings, 17. These sections are followed by footnoes, the data collection instruments and a bibliography. It can be clearly seen that these materials and specifically the three major sections can be easily converted into the first three chapters of the final research report document. In order to convert these sections into chapters, it is obviously necessary to re-write some material and cut out others all together. Beside the obvious use of the research proposal, when completed, parts may be used for progress reports, summary reports and documentation to explain the nature of your project to inquiring interested parties.

The research proposal outline has been designed with topics both major and minor in importance in sequential arrangement that will guide and lead the writer from the basic research ideas to more and more complex and specific topics that provide the necessary detail in order to administer and carry out the research project. Discussion of the sequencing will appear in greater detail in Part III.

THE PROPOSAL OUTLINE IS A REMINDER THAT COMPELS THE USER TO DEAL WITH CERTAIN ISSUES AND TOPICS

The beginning proposal writer is frequently frustrated by not knowing where to begin the writing task. He is equally concerned with anxiety about what should be included and where in the document various information should be located. To put it simply, it is difficult to get beyond that first blank sheet of paper.

The Research Proposal Outline is the answer to the writer's difficulty in getting started. This outline represents a very concrete device for reminding the writer of what topics should normally be dealt with and where they are located in the proposal document. In following this outline closely the writer is compelled to deal with issues and topics he or she might not have thought of during the planning stages of the task. The topics are listed and must be dealt with in some manner. In one sense the outline format stimulates the writer not only to deal with issues and topics but also to elaborate and extend his ideas in greater detail.

FIRST USE AS NOTE TAKING DEVICE

The first recommended use of the research proposal outline is to identify and examine the subheading topics. Once familiarized with the structure and subheading topics the writer can then turn to the notes taken in the first efforts to formulate the research idea. These notes can be sorted out as they may be identified with the subheading topic areas. The notes can be re-examined and edited. Before the process of transcribing your notes to the research proposal outline, four or five copies of the outline should be made. The first copy should be typed on good quality bond paper and the additional copies can be made using a copy machine.

When the transcribing of notes begins, the writer will sense needed improvement in the quality of the notes. Elaborations will quickly be seen as necessary with more editing and more note taking. As each subheading topic area is filled in, the flow and shape of the material will begin to happen. In some topic areas there will be no notes to transcribe or work with, but in other areas the volume of notes will exceed the space available in the proposal outline. In the first instance, more reading and thought will be necessary in order to satisfactorily cover the topics. In the case of an overflow of note material, extra pages may easily be attached to the proposal outline. It is advised at this point that material be carefully edited out while delaying the more severe cutting of material until all notes are transcribed and all topical areas have been covered in some fashion. At this point in time, nothing in the proposal outline is well developed or stylistically perfect; on the contrary, the outline will be a true rough draft.

USING THE PROPOSAL OUTLINE WITH FLEXIBILITY

Up to this point the writer may tend to think that careful and rigorous compliance to the proposal outline is necessary for successful proposal writing using the recommended guidelines. Careful and rigorous work is recommended but at the same time the outline should not be used in a rigid fashion. The outline is an aid to guiding your efforts toward a document that will eventually be used to organize and carry out your research. After all, the research is your invention and innovation and it remains for you to make those decisions that will shape the process of doing the research and the results it produces. If a subheading topic is simply not applicable, then it should be dropped from the outline. Such topics appear in the outline in order to stimulate thought about time. That is, is this or that topic area necessary for discussion and consideration when writing your proposal? Each research project is unique and different, and therefore the requirements of each will be unique and different.

USING SUBHEADINGS AS GUIDE INDICATORS

The frequent use of subheadings makes the writing task flow and develop with ease. It is characteristic of most research writing that topic areas are set off, underlined or otherwise made highly visible. Writing done for other purposes generally does not make such generous use of subheadings and depends on literary style for effective communication. Research writing is not intended to be flowing and poetic rather it is intended to convey a tone of sobriety, objectivity with a paucity of words. One method for achieving this communication is the frequent use of subheadings which kindle the reader's interest and focus his attention each time a new subheading is used. As for the writer, there is less demanding concentration in the development of his ideas because topical areas are expressed by a subheading. When the actual research is near completion and the report writing task begins, the writer is encouraged to write "close" to the data, that is, refrain from esoteric elaboration and dubious colorful interpretation.

The subheading topics suggested in the research proposal outline do not represent the final work in proposal writing. It is recommended that the writer add his own subheading topics as they seem appropriate to his or her project. The writer is also encouraged to revise and re-word any subheading to fit his own sense of appropriateness and writing style. It has been previosuly mentioned that the proposal outline should be used with flexibility, and therefore, molded and drafted to fit the needs of the proposal writer's purposes and objectives.

It is most important for the writer to remember that subheadings as designed in the proposal outline are to serve the purpose of guiding the writer through the necessary steps toward building a sound research project.

MAKE EXTRA COPIES OF THE PROPOSAL OUTLINE

Before any use is made of the research proposal outline, it is highly recommended that several copies of the outline be made as indicated earlier. One copy should be used for transcribing your notes as previously discussed. A second copy should be used for the revisions of first notes and any additional notes and thoughts. A third copy should be used for more stylized writing of the second draft. At this point you may be ready to lift the text of the third draft from the outline format (draft number four). Final proofing of the fourth draft may well lead to a fifth and final copy readied for the sponsor, foundation, advisor or review committee.

USING THE GUIDELINES TO COMPLETE THE PROPOSAL OUTLINE

Part III is composed of specific guidelines that prescribe how each subheading topic may be accounted for and handled. The guidelines in Part III are designed to follow each subheading topic in the exact order as they appear in the research proposal outline in this section (Part II). It is suggested that the writer read and study the material within each subheading topic area of the guidelines at the same time as the notes are being transcribed to the first copy of the outline. This process should lead to the necessary consideration and further deliberation to fulfill the recommended requirements of each topic area. Follow the guidelines and the outline closely and the results should produce a well thought out and comprehensive research proposal.

RESEARCH PROPOSAL OUTLINE

FORMAT

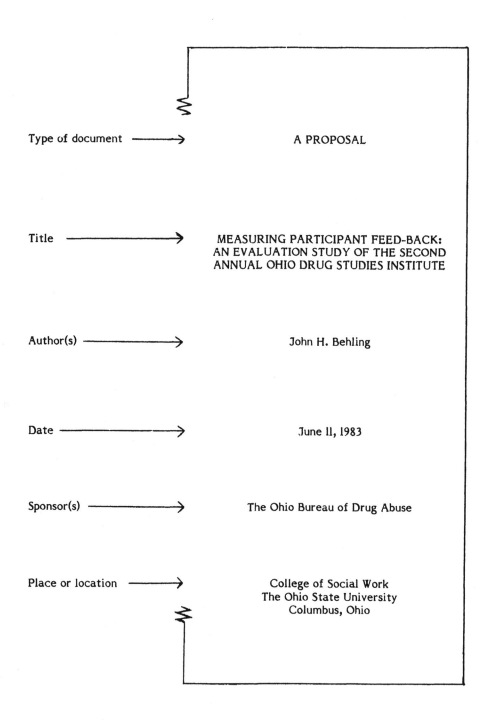

Type of document ⟶   A PROPOSAL

Title ⟶   MEASURING PARTICIPANT FEED-BACK:
AN EVALUATION STUDY OF THE SECOND
ANNUAL OHIO DRUG STUDIES INSTITUTE

Author(s) ⟶   John H. Behling

Date ⟶   June 11, 1983

Sponsor(s) ⟶   The Ohio Bureau of Drug Abuse

Place or location ⟶   College of Social Work
The Ohio State University
Columbus, Ohio

Table of Contents

17

RESEARCH PROPOSAL OUTLINE

SECTION I.   INTRODUCTION

A.   A General Description of the Area of Concern _____

_____

_____

_____

B.   Problems to be Studied _____

_____

_____

_____

_____

_____

C.   Purpose of the Proposed Research Project _____

_____

_____

_____

_____

_____

D.   Major Research Question _____

_____

_____

_____

_____

_____

18

E. Minor Research Questions

    1. _____

_____

_____

    2. _____

_____

_____

    3. _____

_____

_____

    4. _____

_____

_____

    5. _____

_____

_____

    6. _____

_____

_____

F. Major Rearch Hypothesis _____

_____

_____

_____

_____

_____

_____

G. Minor Hypotheses Stating Relationships:

Minor Hypothesis #1 _____

_____

_____

_____

Minor Hypothesis #2 _____

_____

_____

_____

Minor Hypothesis #3 _____

_____

_____

_____

Minor Hypothesis #4 _____

_____

_____

_____

Minor Hypothesis #5 _____

_____

_____

_____

Minor Hypothesis #6 _____

_____

_____

_____

H. Significance of the Problem and Justification for Investigating It _____

_____

_____

_____

_____

_____

_____

_____

_____

_____

_____

_____

I. Feasibility of Doing the Proposed Study _____

_____

_____

_____

_____

_____

_____

_____

_____

_____

SECTION II.   REVIEW OF LITERATURE

A.   Historical Background _____

_____

_____

_____

_____

_____

_____

_____

B.   Theory Relevant to Research Question and Hypotheses _____

_____

_____

_____

_____

_____

_____

C.   Current Literature Relevant to Research Question and Hypotheses _____

_____

_____

_____

_____

_____

_____

_____

SECTION III. METHODOLOGY

A. Restatement of Major or General Hypothesis _____

_____

_____

_____

B. Research Design (Groups to be Compared) _____

_____

_____

_____

_____

_____

_____

C. Draft Schematic Drawing of Research Design: In order to better understand and conceptualize your research project, draw a simple design using circles, or squares or arrows.

D.   General Characteristics of the Study Population_____ __ ____   _____
_____ ____   _____ _____   _____ __ _ _____
_____ _____ ___   _____ _____ _____ _____ _____
_____ __ _____   _____   _____ ___ _____
_____ _____ _____ _____ __ _ _____
_____ __ _____ _____   _____ ____ _____

E.   The Location or Setting in Which Study Takes Place (Indicate where
      respondents were when you collected data from them.)
      The Geographic Dimensions of Study Population_____ __ _ _ ____ ___ ____
_____ ____ ____ _____ __ __ ___ _ _____ ___ _ _____ _ _____
_____ _____ ___ _ __ _____ _____ ___ _____
_____ _____ _ _____ ___ ___ ___ __ _____ ____ _____ ___ _ _____
___ _____ _____ __ _____ ____ _____ _____ __ _ _____
_____ ____ _____ ___ _____ _____ _____ ___ __ _ _ ____ _ _____
_____ _____ __ _____ _____ _ _ _ _____ _____ __ __ __ _____ _ _____

F.   Calendar of Events in Carrying Out Study___ _____ __ _____ __ _____
_____ __ _____ _____ _ __ _____ _____ _____ _____
_____ _ _____ _____ _ _ _____ __ _____ ____ __ ____
_____ _____ _ _____ ___ __ __ _____ __ __ _____ __
__ _____ _____ _____ _____ ____ _____ _____ ___ _ _____
_____ _____ _____ _____ _____ _____ __ ____ _ _____

G.   Sampling Design and Procedures_____ _____ _ _ _____ __ _ ____
____ _____ _____ _____ _____ _____ _____ __ ___ _ _____
_____ __ _ ___ ___ _____ __ _ _____ _____
_____ ___ _ _ _____ __ __ ____
_____ _____ __ _ _____ ____ ____ ___ __ _____ __

24

H. Data Collection Schedule (Questionnaire). List of variables to be measured and identify level of measurement.

1. _____ _____

2. _____

3. _____

4. _____

5. _____

6. _____

7. _____

8. _____

9. _____

10. _____

11. _____

12. _____

13. _____

14. _____

15. _____

I. Instruments, Tools for Measuring Variables--Schedules, and Questionnaires (Scales, Check Lists, Rating Devices, Indexes, Observation Procedures, and Ranking). Make an attachment if additional space is needed.

_____ _____

_____

_____

_____

_____

_____

_____ _____

25

J.   Validity and Reliability _____

_____

_____

_____

_____

_____

K.   Pre-testing the Data Collection Instruments _____

_____

_____

_____

_____

_____

L.   Definition of the Most Important Terms and Concepts Used in the Research Project.

    1. _____

_____

    2. _____

_____

    3. _____

_____

    4. _____

_____

    5. _____

_____

    6. _____

_____

M. Administration of Data Collection Schedule.
(Letter-Persons-Case Records-Situation-TV-Tape)

_____

_____

_____

_____

_____

_____

_____

N. Data Processing Procedures Including Computer Procedures and Coding
Instruction

_____

_____

_____

_____

_____

_____

_____

O. Procedures of Data Analysis: Data Analysis Designs to be Used

_____

_____

_____

_____

_____

_____

_____

P. Special Techniques _____

_____

_____

_____

_____

_____

_____

_____

Q. Human Subject Consideration _____

_____

_____

_____

_____

_____

_____

_____

Attachments:

(1)   Footnotes or references will be placed here. These will be followed by a
       copy of the (2) Data Collection Schedule and (3) a Bibliography.

28

GUIDELINES FOR THE RESEARCH PROPOSAL

It was pointed out in Part II that Part III is divided into three sections that coincide with the three sections of the research proposal outline. These sections are usually entitled Introduction, Review of Literature, and Methodology. Before beginning with the discussion of Section I, "Introduction," it is necessary to give a few words of explanation to the Title Page and the Table of Contents of your proposal.

TITLE PAGE

What information should be placed on the title page? The title page is also referred to as "cover page" and includes the title of the proposed study which is placed in the center of the upper half of the page. The title page should also include the words "A proposal" placed above the title. If the proposal is for a thesis or dissertation, it may read "A THESIS PROPOSAL" or "A DISSERTATION PROPOSAL." Further down the page is the author's full name, below that, the date of the final draft of the proposal, and below that, the name of the institution or organization the author represents. At the bottom of the page, put the place or location of the project. This layout should be made as formal as if it were the final draft. The title of your proposal should express the major or general hypothesis of your study. In the case of survey research, tht title should express the major research question. Titles may be short, two or three words, or long, up to twenty words. This is not important. What is important is the fact that it expresses a clear idea of what is being tested or studied.

TABLE OF CONTENTS

Like the title page, it is important to lay out the table of contents in a formal manner, that is, as if it were the final draft of your work. The table of contents is necessary to your reader or reviewer because frequently readers wish to quickly and easily search out a specific section of the document. The table of contents is used as an index for finding particular material. All chapter or "PART" sections should be included with at least the next level subheading topics included under each Chapter or Part heading. This arrangement would place "Part" first, "Chapter" or "Section" second, and "Subsection" third in order of importance and presentation. Remember to include page numbers after each heading or the table of contents will be of little value to the reader. As for page numbers, be sure the draft is typed in final form before the table of contents is organized and typed.

SECTION I   INTRODUCTION

GENERAL DESCRIPTION OF THE AREA OF CONCERN

It is important to clearly establish the area of concern. Is the problem to be studied adequately related to the larger context in which it is a part? The writer should begin with a broad description of the area. For example, if the problem is "battered wives" it is essential to build an understanding of the area by a discussion of violence and violence within family groups. What is needed is the antecedent and context in which the problem is produced. Social phenomena do not miraculously occur. Events arise from a complex social, economic and psychological fabric. The writer should develop this kind of base before introducing the problem statement. This is not to suggest that a full historical or sociological treatment be developed at this point. A more comprehensive and meticulous tracing should be done in the second section dealing with "Review of Literature." The writer may open this section with a quotation with a historical reference. An anecdote could be cited as a means of setting the tone of area of concern. Reference could be made to specific legislation that is relevant to the problem statement concerning "battered wives."

Generally, this preparatory statement need not be long and involved. One or perhaps two double spaced typewritten pages (on the average there are approximately 250 words typed on each 8½ x 11 inch page) at most should be sufficient to provide the broad context from which the problem statement will emerge. Remember the background statement to the problem will be developed in depth with considerably more elaborate detail in the next section. Here, it is important to convince your reviewer of the fact that you are knowledgeable about the conditions surrounding the problem under consideration. That is, your reader is made aware that you are aware of the connection between the problem to be studied and the wider world.

PROBLEM TO BE STUDIED

The problem statement should first and foremost be expressed as a problem. A problem is a matter of doubt, difficulty or dissatisfaction the answer or solution to which is not immediately evident After all, the problem should be expressed in such a way as to convince its readers that its solution will leave the world a better place in which to live. The writer himself should obviously be convinced of the importance of the problem and its anticipated solution. This importance must be conveyed to the reader or reviewer. Arouse the reader's curiosity by making clear what is in doubt. In stating the problem, the writer should state it in such a way as to capture the reader's interest and attention. The writer should assume that the reviewer though probably a sophisticated person, is not very well informed in the problem area. For this reason alone the refinement of the problem is absolutely necessary. Much time should be taken to define and delineate the problem in order to eliminate doubt in the reviewer's mind as to what exactly is being studied by all the research effort that will follow.

First, it is necessary to explain why the problem is a problem. What is it that is malfunctioning? At this point it might be helpful to document the seriousness of the problem. Second, point out the relationship between the problem and given theory. This need not be well developed here because the review of literature is the place for more careful and extended elaboration of theory. Every problem, like everything else, is related to a larger world. It is important to show the generality of the problem. As the research proposal develops the writer should point out how this research will contribute to a larger body of theory which in turn explains the relationship of a larger number of variables that previously remained isolated and without meaning. When the problem is studied and understood, it should explain a great many doubts and questions. Third, it is difficult to say how long or short the problem statement should be. Do not carry on beyond two or three pages. Make your statement succinct including the theory as it touches the problem and the implications the problem has for those most closely affected. Remember, the review of literature section allows plenty of space for discussing the many facets of the problem and related research.

PURPOSE OF THE PROPOSED RESEARCH PROJECT

The introductory chapter opened with a short discussion of the "general area of concern" followed by a "statement of the problem" followed by "purpose of the proposed research." The writer should be aware that the direction and character of this material begins from a wide and very general presentation to a narrowing of scope as you proceed with the discussion. In this case each topical subheading becomes more specific with each writing.

The statement of purpose is crucial to the project planning simply because every method and procedure flows from it. Simply stated the purpose is the first statement about which the project is all about. Some researchers have used the term "objectives" rather than purpose to describe this section of the proposal. There is no real difference between the two terms "purpose" or "objective." What is being emphasized here is the fact that the two terms should not cause the proposal author confusion.

The statement of purpose should open with one statement followed by several shorter very specific statements of purpose. In both types of statements the reader or reviewer is looking for specific and concrete statements of purpose which are achievable or at least appear to be achievable. The statements should be listed, one or two sentences for each. The several statements should be arranged in order of their importance. If I am studying "battered wives" one purpose may be to see if wives with children resist assault more than wives without children. That is a fairly important question compared to a question concerning the educational level of the battered wife. Yet, it is not unlikely that less important questions may become extremely important once the analysis is completed and the data are interpreted.

Remember to tie the purpose closely to the problem statement that preceded the purpose section. The proposal is a flow of ideas sometimes overlapping but linked together in a chain of reasoning. The importance of the purpose section cannot be overemphasized. In fact, it is the foundation for the remainder of the proposal and the basis of all the work that follows. The whole research effort is predicated on its purpsoe. It sets the stage showing what the researcher intends doing in the way of solving and/or contributing to the solution of the problem. For the critical reviewer who is judging the proposal for the purpose of awarding a possible grant, this purpose section may be the basis for judging the entire project proposal. Again, it is crucial that a clear specific statement or set of statements be made. One of the first things to do when the proposal is complete is to re-read it and make sure that the purpose section smoothly fits with the problem statement. If these sections fit together easily, this will set the stage for the methodology <u>to carry out the prescriptions of the purpose section.</u>

Some researchers, when beginning a career, will lack judgment in a number of areas. So it is important for the researcher to carefully weigh the <u>realistic</u> possibilities of carrying out the research purposes in terms of time, budget, equipment and professional experience needed to do an adequate job. One of the most common errors made by many inexperienced propos al writers is to include statements of purpose within a running description of the project goals. Set them off carefully and clearly. It is equally important to not describe or outline purposes or objectives which will not be carried out by the research procedures later on.

MAJOR RESEARCH QUESTION

The major research question emerges from within the statement of purpose. It should be a clearly stated question that is, in effect, a re-statement of the primary purpose of the research project. The research question is of great importance in guiding the research effort, and for that reason it should be underlined in the text of your proposal. A major research question should be general enough to suggest a great deal of refinement following this section. This refinement or detail will be expressed in the form of "minor research questions" and will be discussed under that subheading. The major research question is also referred to as a "general research question" by some authors. The word "general" implies the broad scope meant to be covered by the question. It might be thought of as an umbrella question which is answered by answering a series of minor questions. For example, a good general question would be "How can human beings live in outer space"? There are hundreds of questions to be asked in order to find a satisfactory answer to the general question.

Much of the research that is done is primarily survey and is therefore concerned with descriptive findings and descriptive answers to research questions. If this is the nature of your research, hypotheses will not be formulated because the testing of relationships is not the purpose of the research. In survey or exploratory research, questions are a more than adequate device for directing the organization of the methodology. If the purpose of the research is to construct a prediction instrument, then the major research question would simply express that end. That is , "can specific social and psychological factors be identified that will be predictive of potential wife battering behavior"? The research would proceed with the collection of data and testing for factor accuracy in predicting the desired outcome.

33

MINOR RESEARCH QUESTIONS

There are a great many possible questions that a researcher may want to ask in order to fully understand an area of interest. However, there is a limit to the number of questions one can ask before the reader is totally distracted from the central purpose of the research. I would suggest that ten or twenty questions would be satisfactory to cover the subject area framed by the major research question. But one cannot be specific about the number of questions without knowing the nature of the project topic.

The questions posed should be <u>specific</u> and clear without reference to value judgement (good and bad). The questions should be specific enought that they can be answerable in specific terms. Philosophical questions should not be posed in this section but should be raised in the very beginnning or in the "Review of Literature" section. Those researchers whose interests focus on survey or exploratory designs will probably present more questions than those testing the hypotheses of an experimental design. The proposal writer should remember that for every question set down in the proposal, a methodological effort will have to be made in order to answer each question. This caution will lead the writer to limit the number of questions set down in some realistic way. Finally, the writer should be aware that the reviewer of his proposal will examine the research questions as means of discovering the extent to which the writer comprehends the subject area being researched. That is, the kinds of questions raised and included in the final draft of the proposal indicate the thoughtfulness of the researcher.

MAJOR RESEARCH HYPOTHESES

Hypotheses are statements that are concerned with the relationship between variables. A major research hypothesis is a restatement of the major research question. Only now the statement expresses the belief in a particular relationship. The hypothesis is the key element of any experimental research project because it states formally what is being investigated and what is expected to be found true under designated conditions. There is always a <u>relationship</u> between two or more concepts stated in a hypothesis. The concept which is believed to be causal in the stated relations becomes the independent variable and the concept believed to be the effect becomes the dependent variable. The hypothesis is a <u>statement</u> of <u>relationship</u> between two variables (concepts) that is in a <u>testable form.</u> The testing of the stated relationsip is the project itself; the procedure of testing is the methodology.

After the hypothesis has been proved true (been verified by the data collected) it becomes a proposition. <u>A proposition, then, is a statement of relationship between two concepts that have been empirically verified.</u> Several related propositions are called <u>theory</u> which explains more generally and abstractly the real world.

Theory is a set of abstract and very general statements supported by propositions (or proven hypotheses) which are specific in their statement of conditons and relationships. In a sense, theory is inseparable from hypotheses since theory is supported by hypotheses and relates to the real world through hypotheses. Single hypotheses are, in a sense, "small theories."

A concise, well conceptualized hypothesis is essential for a research project since it is the focus of all work following its formation. The whole research project depends on the hypothesis since the research process is a formal, detailed test of the relationship between the variables. What then is a hypothesis? It is a question answered. It is a statement of relationship between two variables or empirical events. It is a statement of what one might expect a relationship to be if he had no evidence. Last, it is a positive statement of existence. The value of the hypothesis is that it leads to an empirical test. It is that test that is important, not simply whether the hypothesis is accepted or rejected by evidence.

While the description of the problem is couched in literary terms, hypotheses ought to be couched in operational terms. Of course hypotheses are usually stated in literary terms first, but later must be translated into operational terms. Hypotheses are often stated in the "null" form, i.e., the form that asserts no difference and no relationship, since the statistical tests that will probably be applied are based upon random chance, "no difference" models. Usually, however, this null form does not express the hypothesis as you hope it will turn out. Hypotheses should be stated whereever there is a basis for prediction. That is, when one variable is theoretically related to a second variable presumably the theoretical foundation is well grounded in previous research that the proposal writer has studied and reviewed.

As previously suggested, a researcher is usually interested in setting up a hypothesis which he really would like to reject. The hypothesis which is actually tested is often referred to as a null hypothesis (symbolized as H_0) as contrasted with the research hypotheses (H_1) which is set up as an alternative to H_0. Usually, although not always, the null hypothesis states that there is no difference between several groups or no relationship between variables, whereas the research hypothesis may predict either a positive or negative relationship. The researcher may actually expect that the null hypothesis is faulty and should be rejected in favor of the alternative H_1. The use of the null hypothesis does have one very practical use. It forces the researcher to find out what his data would be like if there were no difference or relationship between variables. In effect the researcher uses the null form in order to neutralize his own bias regarding outcome.

The following set of statements are recommended for the beginning proposal writer for designing good hypotheses (Good and Hatt, 1952: 67-73):

1. A hypothesis should be specific.
2. A hypothesis should have an empirical referent.
3. A hypothesis should be conceptually clear in terms of common definitions.
4. A hypothesis should be testable by available techniques.
5. A hypothesis should be related to a body of theory.

MINOR HYPOTHESES

The previous discussion has described the structure and function of the hypotheses with reference to the major hypothesis in particular. Minor hypotheses are designed in the same manner as the major hypothesis. But how are they

35

different? There will usually be a larger number of minor hypotheses. It is possible to have more than one major hypothesis, perhaps two because both might be considered vital and equally important to the research endeavor. One could design a minor hypothesis for each research question but this is not necessarily so, especially if some research questions are requesting descriptive answers such as "how much" and "how many." These kinds of questions cannot be transformed into hypothesis form.

Finally, it is important to be prepared in the process of doing your research to actually test all the hypotheses you have set down in the research proposal. In fact, it is quite common for researchers to informally test a great many more hypotheses than are actually charged to the research effort. This is a consequence of the use of computer analysis of data. The capacity of the computer to analyze data is so awesome that it would take longer to write out all the hypotheses tested by the computer than all the person hours put into the entire research project including the writing of the research proposal.

SIGNIFICANCE OF THE PROBLEM AND THE JUSTIFICATION FOR ITS INVESTIGATION

How important is it to get answers to the research questions or hypotheses? There are at least two audiences that will be directly or indirectly affected by your research. First, there is the researcher and those associated with the project. Second, the wider world that is unassociated with the project. The first group will be concerned with building new knowledge and contributing to an already existing body of knowledge. The second audience is equally important as a justification for investigating the problem. There may be a large number of individuals directly affected by the results of your research, such as the "battered wives" project. Evidence strongly suggests that a serious problem exists and research is needed to better understand this phenomenon and its causes. In this example, wives are the population most seriously affected by whatever research may be done. Will this research improve the situation? Millions of dollars have been spent on research into the causes, treatment and rehabilitation of cancer and cancer patients. The continued effort in cancer research seems worthwhile considering the suffering that patients must endure. To those suffering from wife battering and cancer, any kind of improvement in their situation may be weighed as a significant positive step. There are long enduring problems that remain with us that continue to need study. One such problem is crime and its victims. There are problems that have immediate popularity and garner enormous public attention and willingness to heavily finance research efforts to deal with them. Such a problem is the so-called "drug problem" of the late sixty's and early seventy's. The solution to this problem has great significance for the general public. Some problems are far too theoretical and abstract to have any kind of immediate impact on a large general public. Improving counseling services to those experiencing sexual dysfuncton is not a well established field of practice. The improvement of effectiveness in this area may not be a highly visual demand being made by a highly vocal public but it remains an area of needed expertise. Some research has a large following, both professional and general public, while other research has a very limited audience of enthusiastic followers and supporters. This does not mean that one should be supported with generous funding and the other totally ignored. It does mean that the justification is different and must be stated in the research proposal . After all, the popular support of certain research efforts is in no way related to the success in building or advancing new knowledge in that area. Nor does it mean the quality of research will be affected by level of popularity among scientists and laymen. It remains important that research that has limited popular support is not neglected but needs a different kind of justification in order to clear away obstacles from its development.

Finally, it is necessary for the writer to express his or her own feeling about the importance and significance of the proposed research. How strongly are you committed to this project? If the project is simply an obscure investigation of some esoteric idea lost for the most part in some remote volume hidden away in a dusty library, it still has value for the investigator. In all such cases express personal and professional reasons for its study. Far too many graduate students and some experienced researchers seem to be only mildly interested in their research ideas. If the creator of an idea is indifferent to its investigation, how can one expect others to be enthusiastic about it. Some researchers feel it is important to let others generate enthusiasm for their ideas so that they remain aloof and objective. I say nonsense. Show your commitment through a careful description of your concern.

FEASIBILITY OF DOING THE PROPOSED STUDY

Every researcher and every would be researcher has casually outlined a "dream" project over cops of coffee. As a matter of fact there are hundreds and hundreds of splendid ideas and exciting projects discussed by old research hands as well as starry-eyed novices. One of the reasons that few, very few of these ideas even get beyond the talking stage is their feasibility. First of all, there is simply not enough time to plan, carry out, analyze and distribute the end products of so many potential projects. All researchers plot, plan and dream from time to time, but few ideas are ever turned into reality.

When a researcher starts devoting the time and energy to writing a proposal for a "dream" idea you can be sure that he is seriously considering the project as an endeavor. It is at this stage of the project that proposal writers should consider the feasibility of makng a considerable investment of time and energy to a project. At the proposal writing stage a serious amount of thought should be given to whether or not the project is worth all the effort it will require for completion. Graduate students frequently do not weigh this matter carefully enough. Far too many never finish their projects once begun. Do I really want to do this project? A simple question requiring a long and thoughtful answer.

How much time is required to do this work and is it too much of an investment? What are your time constraints? Will there be enough time to finish the project? What will be the cost of the project? What are the costs to the researcher and what investment in terms of dollars are there for the materials to carry out the project? Do you have to employ interviewers? Will the coding and processing costs be too much? How much of this work can you do on your own? If the proposal is being written for a grant, costs should be carefully enumerated as

37

part of the grant request. For those graduate students seeking acceptance of a research proposal the problem of feasibility is a more serious issue. Grant proposals can be expanded to include in the research operation necessary resources broadening feasibility.

If the research envisioned includes travel beyond the home of the researcher, graduate student researchers may have difficulty traveling frequently to the location where the research is carried on. Again, there is cost and time involved with travel and may be a limiting factor. It is important to examine each possible limiting factor by spelling out the issue of feasibility. Far too many projects have terminated before completion and therefore represent a considerable loss of resources and patience of anxious graduate students. Perhaps by the time the proposal writer reaches the feasibility section of the proposal outline, he will have decided to take up an entirely new vocation.

There is some debate as to the exact nature of a review of literature insofar as hypothesis building is concerned. Some researchers have argued that hypotheses are formulated before the review of literature formally begins. Other researchers have argued that the hypotheses that guide the research effort are derived from the review of literature. This writer has been impressed with both arguments but tends to favor the former argument while using the review of literature to strengthen previously designed hypotheses and building additional hypotheses. But regardless of the priori or a priori design of hypotheses the review of literature builds depth and understanding around the primary hypotheses of the research. In the case of survey designs where research questions are used to guide the research, the review of literature is used to develop additional questions and deepen the researcher's understanding of the area of concern and the specific problem to be studied.

The purpose of this section of the research proposal is to review all the known literature relevant and related to the problem to be studied. It is almost essential that the proposal writer become a minor expert in the area of concern. At least he can become sufficiently knowledgeable about the area to describe the primary characteristics of the problem area, to quote the major authors in the area, to enumerate the relevant facts about the problem, to outline the history of the problem and discuss the major and minor theories explaining the problem and its impacting consequences. It is obvious that the review of literature could be very extensive. In some projects it absorbs a good deal of space as well as occupying a great deal of the researcher's time. In the case of "library" research where secondary sources are used, the entire thesis or dissertation can be composed of "review of literature" material. The review of literature section may and more often than not will comprise the longest section in the research proposal. This points up another value to writing a research proposal, that is, the opportunity to develop a review of literature in the proposal that is ninety percent complete and ready to be transformed into the final research report. Obviously there will be some revisions and modifications necessary between the time the proposal is written and the actual research is completed. The only exception to this happy situation is the case study or historical thesis or dissertation. In such instances only an outlining of primary authors and their theories would be needed in the "review of literature" section of the research proposal.

The review of literature is sometimes viewed as a "dirty chore" or at best an uninteresting requirement demanded by aging professors. Some students see it as contributing little or nothing to the overall proposal task. To be sure, the literature review has several real uses. First, it demonstrates to the advisor or proposal reviewer that the proposal writer has comprehensive understanding of the area of concern and a reasonable knowledge of the important and essential information which is relevant to the problem to be studied. Second, it gives the writer a foundation upon which to build knowledge. To be sure, it is absolutely silly and wasteful to "re-discover the wheel." Students are forever saying they cannot find any research or literature regarding a specific problem. Nine times out of ten this is not true. As mentioned earlier the writer must become an expert in his area of study. This means he must become conversant with most of the literature related to the problem. This, when once achieved, will show a competence in the area being studied. Third, a good review of literature will enable you to show just how your study will refine, revise and extend what is already known. Remember research is a serious business so it is important to stop fighting your problem by avoiding a solid and comprehensive review of literature. One of the very first questions a reviewer will ask is "Is there an adequate review of the literature?" In short, a literature reviewer tells you what others have done or are doing in your problem area. It will answer many questions you have raised and will produce many new questions you had not thought of prior to the search. The search is the foundation for making your methodology more specific in terms of procedures of study which will be spelled out in great detail in the methodology section of the proposal.

The review of literature section recommended in the outline is oranized into three major subheadings: Historical Background, Theory Relevant to the Major Research Question, and Current Literature. The writer is reminded to follow the outline, but at all times modify the recommendations if necessary to fit the unique nature of the problem to be studied. Put very simply, be flexible in the use of the outline.

HISTORICAL BACKGROUND

Everything has an antecedent. To begin to investigate any problem or pursue any interest it is likely that one would trace that problem or interest to its deeper origins. But where are the origins of any problem? The process appears to have no end, that as one dimension leads to another, another dimension is soon to follow, and another and another like an endless chain of complex links each as fascinating as the last. The issue involved with the tracing of any problem or interest is to identify each nexus where a departure becomes apparent. This discussion sounds very much like the kind of thinking that the historian would pursue in developing an outline for his historical research problem. But non-historical projects are equally concerned with historical origins, yet not to the extent that the historian may be. Every act has its antecedents and they need to be understood by the researcher in order to properly comprehend the theoretical base that explains the existence of the problem.

In writing your proposal, it is essential that a statement of facts about the problem be included. This inclusion should be shaped into a historical re-training of important events. The writer should clearly convey a knowledge of the origins by accurately identifying significant dates and events. Obviously these dates and events should be relevant to the research problem. They should give a context that adds a background of social signficance.

In the process of digging up your facts (dates and events relevant to the problem) be sure to strengthen your writing with supporting documentation whenever available and quotable. In regard to supporting evidence, be sure to use every possible source including personal interviews with authorities in the field.

It may be helpful if the proposal writer would simply arrange dates and events in a chronological order and begin to trace each event one to another. The entire historical background need not be an elaborate historical treatise, especially for the master's thesis research proposal. An historical tracing of the research problem should include the proper identification of important and significant persons closely associated with the problem area. These persons may be relatively "famous" or relatively unknown to those outside the field of interest. At any rate be sure that the "good guys" and "bad guys" are properly included with the flow of significant dates and events. Always give credit where credit is due.

It is also likely that you will want to include a reporting of some of the earlier research done in the problem area. That is, some research may have historical value more than theoretical soundness; for example, earlier theories of mental illness propounding the infestation of evil spirits as the cause of insanity. This theory has no scientific validation but gives historical meaning to the problem as it exists today. Naturally, one should include notorious research as well as theories of an earlier origin. After all, many of the earlier theories were the result of deductive thinking rather than inductive research, but still add much to the historical context being developed.

If the historical section ends up being much too long, there is no reason why it cannot be edited and re-written.

THEORY RELEVANT TO THE MAJOR RESEARCH QUESTION

In this section the writer is expected to examine theory relevant to the investigation described in the proposal. If there is any theoretical base for the study it should be developed and laid out in this section. Later, when the project is carried out and the findings are being written into the final document, the writer should return to the material presented here regarding theoretical base. The new data or new findings from the research should be integrated into the established theory base. This, as you might guess is called "Systematically contributing to the field's knowledge base." But let us begin by examining the term theory.

What is a theory? Theories are explanations of how and why things happen the way they do. Theories interrelate individual findings from many single-purpose pieces of research. With the vast amount of different kinds of research in progress at all times, there is an ongoing need to constantly be integrating research findings, old and new, conclusive and inconclusive into new theoretical frameworks. Selltiz and company describe theory in the following way: "In general, however, the intention of a theory in modern science is to summarize existing knowledge, to provide an explanation for observed events and relationships on the basis of the explanatory principles embodied in the theory." (Selltiz, et al., 1959: 481)

In the beginning of your work, before the writing of the proposal has been started, your examination of the literature should be fairly general. As you catalog each reading, the focus will become more precise and narrowed. In this process be sure to note references that are usually scattered throughout each reading. Examine footnotes carefully. Footnotes are an excellent source for leading you to additional sources. Continue this process and your various connections to the problem to be studied will increase and thereby broaden your own understanding of the area of concern. When do you know that you have covered all the relevant material? The process of reviewing research and research findings will eventually lead you back to the same references. That is, in time your readings will be quoting readings you have already encountered and catalogued. In a real sense you will have traced your subject in a circle of authors and references. In this process, footnotes will become familiar to you. When this begins to happen, you will know that the relevant literature is being covered by your search.

When the writing begins, it is imperative that relevant research should be summarized. During this process of summarizing you may find it helpful to narrow your focus to five or six sources that you consider to be most important to your problem. Some authors and researchers may prove to be experts in the area. Their works should be even more closely examined for relevance to your proposed project. Once you have narrowed your concentration to a few vitally important sources, you may begin to relate your problem to this material. This can be done by raising questions in the text of your writing as if you were talking with these authors and researchers. It may appear to be a group discussion led by you regarding your particular subject of interest. This effort will include the organizing of material (authors, researchers, theories) so that theoretical statements appear logical and thereby revealing obvious gaps in the knowledge structure. This gives you the opportunity to present your own ideas and theoretical contributions. In this process you may very well present opposing and conflicting points of view. So much the better. If there are conflicts and they are well documented, let them stand. Your contribution may well resolve some of this difference or create more conflicting points for further argument.

CURRENT LITERATURE

Reviewing literature that dates back many years is obviously a necessary and important task and has been discussed in the preceding section. But there should be special emphasis placed on the very latest research and literature. It is the judgment of this writer that of all the material related to a research problem, the most significant is probably the current literature. It is significant because it represents material that is the product of the very lastest techniques, methods, data analysis technology and statistical tests. For example, twenty years ago when this writer was a graduate student, the two statistical tests most used and considered to be the most accurate and precise probability tests of signficance were chi square for nominal data and Pearson's Correlation coefficient for interval data. Many new data analysis designs have been developed since that time. Research and literature being published now are based on these new techniques and provide us with greater confidence in research findings. It is for this reason among others that current literature should deserve your most careful consideration.

In your search for current literature, you will obviously find links to the past but one must search different sources to find current material. For example, a great deal of research is at this moment in progress and not available for publication, let alone available to your searching eyes. Much material is not in published form, but is complete and waiting for some form of communication process to carry it into the streams of intellectual debate. Given these problems of availability, the researcher must make all his connections on a primary basis.

The researcher may "hear" of some fellow researcher doing work related to his problem area. Correspondence by letter, or better yet, by long distance telephone will produce a congenial response and a large package of mimeographed reading material. Researchers are almost always willing to share what they have in the way of findings and significant results. Most important to this kind of search is the need to talk to as many people as possible at all levels of academic and non-academic life. You can be sure that it will produce current material and ideas that will contribute significantly to your research proposal writing task and ultimately to your project and its anticipated satisfactory completion. You should be willing to share your ideas with others that have been kind enough to share their hard won research findings with you. Ideally, a network of scholarly individuals should develop giving each writer a sense of belonging to a community of scientists concerned with solving society's problems. That sounds lofty and unrealistic, but this writer continues to strive for that kind of learning environment.

By the time you have started running into the same authors and the same articles and the same ideas you can begin to feel confident that you have covered the literature relevant to your problem. Another sure way to recognize that you have covered all bases is your own sense of expertness. Are you now capable of arguing with others who are acknowledged as experts in the field? If you feel you can (with some confidence) then you have probably covered all the relevant literature in your problem area.

Finally, your research proposal should reflect a summary of major and some minor articles that clearly demonstrate to your advisor or proposal reviewer a high quality proposal and a competent researcher.

SECTION III   METHODOLOGY

The purpose of this section is to present the methods by which the proposed study will be carried out. The greater the detail and care taken in the preparation of this section, the more efficiently and easily the research will be completed. All steps will go according to the plan if the plan is carefully and meticulously organized. If the previous two sections of the proposal were announced as important to the proposal, this section should be considered even more important.

Why is this section important and useful to the researcher? The "Methods" or "Procedures" section (many researchers use the title heading "Procedures" or "Methods" in the place of "Methodology") is a specific set of procedures that direct the researcher in the administration of the project. Almost all of the material in this section of the proposal should be transferred to the "Methodology" chapter in the final research report. Science is based on replication, that is the capacity to validate a piece of research by using the same methods of study. In the presentation of any research findings, the methods by which these results were obtained must be also presented with the findings. The methodology is, in fact, the authority base for the research. When the researcher reveals his methods through publication, he challenges his critics to question, to doubt or to reject his findings. In effect, the findings (the content) are only as good as the methods used to produce the findings. Those researchers who refuse or avoid revealing their methods or sources of information sacrifice their credibility because if the methods for producing results cannot be made available for close scrutiny, then such results are assumed to lack validity. Again, the methods or source is as important as the actual results making one inexorably tied to the other. It is for these reasons that a complete and comprehensive methodology section be included in the research proposal. Too many students write far too little about their research methods in the proposal as well as the final research report. Sponsors of research are skeptical of data when little or no information regarding methods is given in the report document and the same is equally true of the proposal. The writer runs far less risk of criticism in writing too much in the methods section of the proposal as compared to the other sections of the proposal. Science and research (research is the action arm of science) are founded on systematic methodology. Therefore, the right to replicate any research is a right available to all who are so inclined to attempt replication. In a very real sense, the methods section is similar to a recipe from a cookbook; anyone can get the same results using the same recipe if procedures are systematically and carefully followed.

The logical arrangement of subject headings in this section of the research proposal tends to follow the logic of the research process. The section opens with a restatement of the major hypothesis (or hypotheses) or question. Next, the appropriate research design followed by a description of the population to be studied is inserted. This is followed by a discussion of instruments for measuring variables and a pretest exercise, the collection of data and the necessary procedures involved in the collection of data, methods of data processing and finally data analysis designs to produce and answer the charge embodied in the hypotheses or research questions. Let us beign with the restatement of the major research hypothesis or question.

44

RESTATEMENT OF THE MAJOR RESEARCH HYPOTHESIS OR QUESTION

The restatement of your hypothesis or question at this point in the proposal is necessary to remind the reader or reviewer that all the methods discussed in this section are focused on answering the test set up by the hypothesis or question. This statement should be absolutely clear in the minds of everyone concerned. The reader and writer will be making continual reference to the major hypothesis or question because all hinges on that statement or question. That is, no other statement or question is more important.

RESEARCH DESIGN

What do we mean by "research design" and why is it so important to discuss in the research proposal? A good design will identify the control of those primary variables under investigation. Researh design clearly identified which variables are expected to produce the experiemntal effect (independent variables) and which will be measures of it (dependent variables). Research design means the ordering and the arrangement of observations for the purpose of identifying variables that cause, influence, relate, associate and/or affect in some way other variables. Design is a structuring of systematic observation to investigate the influence of one variable or a group of variables on a given situation, condition and/or other variable. Design is an attempt to methodologically trap an answer to your hypothesis or question. The goal of research design is to establish a predictable influence (cause-effect or independent-dependent nexus) between well defined and specific variables (Polansky, 1974, 38-39).

Before examining the many different kinds of research designs, it is important to consider the differences between studies based on secondary sources and primary sources. The former is sometimes referred to as "library" research. In planning a research project the source of the data shapes the character of the work to be done. Much research is carried out using secondary or library data. This is the kind of research that is written almost entirely as a review of literature. The principle difference between library and other types of research is that the numbers of cases used to support a hypothesis in non-library research are taken from direct observatrion while library research is based on collecting and organizing pieces of research that support or reject a given hypothesis. Library research is obviously far more qualitative than non-library studies. Among the different types of library studies we would classify the philosophical analysis, the case study, historical studies, and some exploratory studies. Scholars and researchers use the library approach when attempting to write articles for publication based on secondary sources. Of course, many formally published studies are based on primary-direct observation data. More will be said about these qualitative studies later in this section.

Chart A

RESEARCH DESIGN

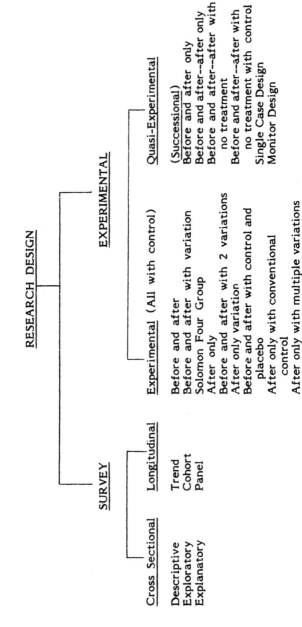

SURVEY

Cross Sectional

Descriptive
Exploratory
Explanatory

Longitudinal

Trend
Cohort
Panel

EXPERIMENTAL

Experimental (All with control)

Before and after
Before and after with variation
Solomon Four Group
After only
Before and after with 2 variations
After only variation
Before and after with control and
    placebo
After only with conventional
    control
After only with multiple variations

Quasi-Experimental

(Successional)
Before and after only
Before and after--after only
Before and after--after with
    no treatment
Before and after--after with
    no treatment with control
Single Case Design
Monitor Design

46

Research designs may be classified into two major types: Survey and Experimental designs. Survey designs do not have control group comparison nor is there any independent or "cause" variable. Experimental designs always have an independent or cause variable present and a control group. Some designs have no control group comparison at all; these are referred to as quasi-experimental designs. Chart A shows the classification of the two major classes and variations flowing from each.

In order to more explicitly illustrate types of designs, each design is schematically laid out to show the dimensions of time, independent variable and observations.

I.   SURVEY DESIGNS

The survey designs are observations taken at one or more points in time. There is no reference to a control group control nor independent variable.

   1.   Cross-Sectional Surveys

Descriptive	▢	one time only observation
Exploratory	▢	one time only observation
Explanatory	▢	one time only observation

All three cross-sectioned designs are observation at one time only. The descriptive design is used for community surveys such as need assessment projects. The exploratory design is used to accumulate data in order to formulate more precise hypotheses and research questions. Explanatory designs attempt to make assertions about the population being studied (Babbie, 1973: 58). The researcher may want to explain the relationship of one variable to a second variable and would use an explanatory design. This process requires at least a bivariate analysis, if not a multivariate analysis of the survey data.

   2.   Longitudinal Surveys

Some surveys allow for the analysis of data at different points in time. A descriptive or explanatory survey may be carried out at a second and third time or more in order to see changes over time. These are not experimental because no causal factor is assumed to be operating in the survey situation. Longitudinal designs are trend, cohort and panel.

Trend $\boxed{T_1}$ $\boxed{T_2}$ $\boxed{T_3}$

Each set of observations is a different sample.

Cohort $\boxed{T_1}$ $\boxed{T_2}$ $\boxed{T_3}$

Each set of observations is a different sample but from the same population.

Panel $\boxed{T_1}$ $\boxed{T_2}$ $\boxed{T_3}$

Each set of observations are taken from the same sample at three different times.

II. EXPERIMENTAL DESIGNS

Experimental designs vary greatly but have one characteristic in common. All such designs have a cause or independent variable present in the study arrangement. Many experimental designs have control groups which greatly strengthen the researchers ability to isolate the causal connection between the independent and dependent variables. Some quasi-experimental designs do not include a control group and are therefore much weaker designs. Designs with a non-random selected control group are sometimes referred to as non-experimental designs.

Definition of symbols:

$\square$	=	Observation
$\boxed{B}$	=	Before observation
$\boxed{A}$	=	After observation
X	=	Independent Experimental Variable
_	=	Independent Control Variable

1. The Classic Before and After Design

This is the best design of all. There is an experimental group and a control group with a before and after set of observations.

2. The Classic Before and After with Two Experimental Variation Groups

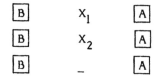

This is a more complex form of the classic design. A second experimental variable is included making a third group with before and after observations.

48

3. Solomon Four Group

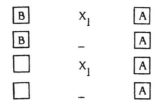

This is even a more complex form of the classical before and after design. What this design achieves is the testing of "pretest" effects as can be seen in pretest for two groups and no pretest for two additional groups. It is the most rigorous design one can use, but it is difficult to organize because of the large number of case needed for the four groups.

4. Before and After with Experimental Variation

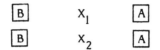

This is the classic design, but without a true control group for contrast. The treatment X_2 variable is of a different type from the X_1 variable.

5. Before and After with control and <u>Placebo</u> Groups

This design includes the classic before and after observations with control and a third group that is given the Placebo.

6. The After-Only

No before observation is taken but both groups have treatment (experimental) and no treatment (control) variables present.

7. The After-Only with Conventional Treatment as Control

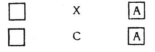

There are no before observations and no control group present. Conventional treatment is given the second group.

49

8. The After-Only with Experimental Variation

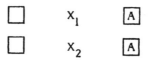

There is no true control group to compare with the experimental group.

9 The After Only Design with Multiple Experimental Variation Groups

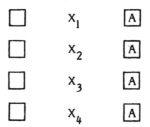

There is no true control group present for this design. There are many experimental groups that may be compared. There is no before observation.

III. QUASI-EXPERIMENTAL DESIGNS

Under the general classification of quasi-experimental designs there are three types: successional, single case and monitor. These three designs have in common some form of experimental or independent variable and three or more sets of observations through time. There is one notable exception and that is the before and after design with treatment variable (independent) between the two observations.

Successional Designs

1. Before and After $\boxed{B}$ X $\boxed{A}$

No control group is present but a treatment variable is present.

2. Before and After--After Only $\boxed{B}$ X $\boxed{A_1}$ X $\boxed{A_2}$

There is no control group but the design has two treatment experiences before and after the second set of observations.

3. Before and After--After--After Only

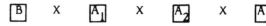

There is no control group present but there are three treatment variable experiences present.

50

4. Before and After--After No Treatment

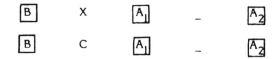

There is no control group present and only one treatment variable experience with a control time lapse period following the second set of observations.

5. Before and After--After with Conventional and Control Group

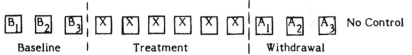

This design has a control group with an aided set of observations after a control time lapse period for both experimental and control groups.

Single Case Design

$$\boxed{B_1}\ \boxed{B_2}\ \boxed{B_3}\ \Big|\ \boxed{X}\ \boxed{X}\ \boxed{X}\ \boxed{X}\ \boxed{X}\ \boxed{X}\ \Big|\ \boxed{A_1}\ \boxed{A_2}\ \boxed{A_3}\quad \text{No Control}$$

Baseline | Treatment | Withdrawal

This design makes use of only one case that is observed at many different points through time. There is no control case although one could be added (Johnson, 1977).

Monitor Design

$$\boxed{B}\ \boxed{B}\ \boxed{B}\ \boxed{B}\ \boxed{B}\ \boxed{B}\ \boxed{B}\quad X\quad \boxed{A}\ \boxed{A}\ \boxed{A}\ \boxed{A}\ \boxed{A}\ \boxed{A}$$

The monitor research design is another Quasi-Experimental design. It is similar to the single case design having no control case. The monitor design has only a series of before observations of the one case (subject) and one set of after observations. The design presumes that some experimental variable is introduced at some midpoint in the monitoring process (Sammon, 1975).

SPECIAL NOTES ON SINGLE CASE DESIGNS

Because this monograph has been organized around the study of problems concerned with large numbers of cases or nomothetic research, a special section is provided to focus on the study of single cases or ideographic research.

This is a brief description of single case research and an explanation as to how to carry out such a monitoring project. Let us begin by dividing this discussion into two parts: (1) a definition of single case research, and (2) a discussion as to its actual application. There are many different kinds of research methods, techniques, strategies and designs available for the study and analysis of problems. The single case design embodies a strategy that is applicable to the study of a single case. In particular, the researcher may study himself or herself in order to maintain a specific behavior or change a specific behav or. Within the single case design there is a further refinement referred to as "monitoring" which is particularly suited to the practitioner s work setting. It is this design that we will describe here.

Monitor research is the systematic observation of a specific behavior or set of behaviors over a period of time (duration). The observation is expected to be stardardized in the measurement of behavior or activity. The observer may well be observing himself or herself (self monitoring) or someone else or some non human target behavior activity (external monitoring). A schedule should be designed to include instruments to measure the observed target behavior. Copies of this schedule should be constructed in such a fashion that easy access be afforded the data collection process. The monitor design is classified within single case design because only one unit of study is observed (the case) on a series of different points through time. The pattern created by these observations is analyzed for change through time and in relation to an introduced (intervening) or experimental variable. Monitor designs include the major features of time series analysis which is common to the study of economic data. An experimental dimension of the monitor design is added when an intervening (experimental) variable "X" is introduced after the establishment of baseline behavior. The use of an intervening variable is optional and need not be planned or introduced at all. This distinguishes monitor designs from single case designs. However, monitoring behavior tends to produce a change in behavior as a result of observing it. This is referred to as "reactivity." This is sometimes a desired effect and is encouraged in certain kinds of enterprises such as weight loss programs and cigarette smoking reduction efforts. More often than not, the self-monitored behavior will be accompanied by a treatment or experimental variable. This will be followed by a period of continued observation and data collection of the target behavior or set of behaviors. The design is summarized in the following illustration:

experimental variable
B_o = observations before the introduction of X variable

$B_o B_o B_o B_o B_o B_o B_o X \ A_o A_o A_o A_o A_o A_o A_o A_o A_o A_o$
A_o = observations after the introduction of X variable.

One can begin work on a monitor project by selecting a problem for study. Two common problems that we might use for illustrative purposes is the need to lose weight and the need to stop or reduce cigarette smoking. Begin by asking questions that seem to be related to the problem. For example, how many calories a day do you consume? What kinds of food do you consume? When do you consume what you consume? How do you feel emotionally when you consume food? When you have written fifteen or twenty questions, you are ready to select and screen out those questions least relevant. Type these statements on a neat format. The format should be convenient and easy to use. You must work out all the possible categories (answers) for each question. These categories should be placed by or under each question to be checked when appropriate.

Begin by identifying the target behavior and the time frame in which it occurs. You may want to observe and record (collect) information once each day. It is possibly you may want to record every occasion that this behavior would occur. It you were studying a client in counseling and you wished to determine the level of attitude change or behavior change, you would record data after each counseling session. At any rate, data are gathered on a separate schedule for each day or occurrence.

When you have established a baseline of behavior (6 to 10 observations), you will be ready to introduce an intervening variable. The introduction of the intervening variable will presumably affect the target behavior (smoking or weight). At this point you will want to maintain the presence of the intervening variable for 6 to 10 observation periods. After that series, you have the choice of either continuing the presence of the intervening variable or withdrawing it and continuing to observe the target behavior (weight and cigarettes smoked) for another 6 to 10 observation period.

When you have neared the end of your period of experimentation and/or monitoring, you will want to begin processing your data and selecting an appropriate data analysis design. One of the best methods for determining significance of change is the technique of graphing. By graphing we mean plotting each data point on graph paper as illustrated below.

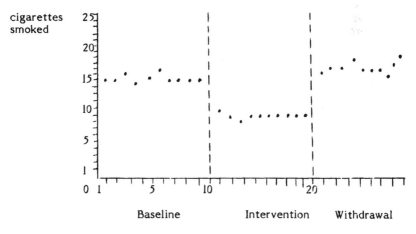

It is apparent that a reduction in smoking has occurred during the intervention phase. The researcher now assumes that the intervention has had some impact on the target behavior.

This discussion should give you some idea of the character of single case designs The preparation of a proposal to carry out such a design will be quite unique when compared to the many nomothetic designs discussed in this monograph.

SCHEMATIC DRAWING OF RESEARCH DESIGN

The subsection on research design has been represented by a series of schematic drawings of different designs. Many students are unable to communicate clearly the nature of their research problem. In order to better conceptualize the writer's understanding of his project, it is advisable to lay out the research design as represented in the drawings in the last subsection. A drawing as illustrated in the previous subsection should be most helpful to the readers of your proposal. Be sure to indicate in your drawing the independent and dependent variables. The drawing should include notations and indications of set of observations, time sequences, and the direction of activity and labeled variables.   In the preparation of the drawing the writer will more clearly understand his problem as well as more easily aid his reviewer in conceptualizing the research design.

CLASSICAL BEFORE AND AFTER (WITH CONTROL GROUP) DESIGN

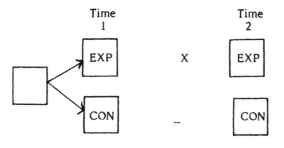

X = Experimental or intervening variable

GENERAL CHARACTERISTICS OF THE STUDY POPULATION

Why write a description of the population to be studied? The reviewer or advisor of your proposal cannot judge the relevance of your project without knowing at least the general characteristics of those persons in the study. It is quite likely that the population will be so unique that the project is not feasible, given the limits of the proposal writer's monetary means. One of the first questions to be answered by a researcher is "who is being studied"? It would be more interesting if one could study beings from outer space but such a study is impossible inasmuch as no one can seem to identify any such creatures. If one were to do a study of power structures with a focus on medium size cities as the units of study one would be expected to spend a great deal of time describing in detail each city to be surveyed and analyzed. If one were concerned with matching cases from two different geographical locations, knowing the characteristics would be absolutely necessary in order to pair-match cases from each location.

Some amount of information is necessary to know early on in the planning and proposal writing stage of the project. If one is to study the aging process, one would presumably want to examine persons from different age groupings. It is therefore important that a detailed description of your study population be presented in the research proposal. If the unit of study is the human being, then some general characteristics seem necessary to report. These common characteristics of value to the reader are age, sex, occupation, race, geographic location, length of residence, income level, and education. Each proposed project will require some unique descriptors. For example, if one were studying cancer patients in a counseling program, the health of the patient would be a most relevant characteristic to include in the proposal. Other kinds of information about the patient would be equally important such as size of family, date of diagnosis, type of treatment being given, type of cancer and the general and specific prognosis. Every population has (a) a set of general characteristics and (b) a specific set of characteristics unique to the population being studied.

LOCATION OR SETTING IN WHICH THE STUDY TAKES PLACE

Why is the location of the study important? Why should it be discussed in the research proposal? Not unlike the previous subsection on describing the population to be studied, the location greatly determines the feasibility of the entire project. If the location requires extensive travel then costs will have to be considered and may delay the project beyond realistic dates of completion. For example, a project may require special equipment such as a soundproof room equipped with a twoway glass and playroom toys. This type of setting would be difficult to procure. Such a setting is rarely found but on a college campus and permission may be difficult to obtain for its use. Another example of special setting problems is the need for special measuring devices. The construction of some devices may require special skills, and finding and employing such skill takes time and money. These are more reasons for delay and possible postponement of the project. For these reasons the proposal writer should carefully describe the location or setting of the project. This includes geographic location as well as the nature of the setting. Such descriptions may well include social agencies, a school, files in a bureaucracy, a community, medical clinics. The uniqueness of the location or setting must be clearly laid out and detailed.

CALENDAR OF EVENTS IN CARRYING OUT STUDY

Why prepare a calendar of events? A calendar of events is a time schedule for carrying out the required tasks of the research project. It represents more of the detailed organization necessary for convincing your advisor or reviewer that the project is indeed feasible. The time schedule or calendar is another indication of how carefully and realistically the proposal has been developed. Very often a reviewer may have difficulty following the flow of your material and when he turns to the calendar of events, he will be able to find the clarification that he has been looking for all along. The calendar logically follows a sequence of events that parallel the research process and in fact embodies the research process to a great extent.

Specific dates should be set for the completion of various tasks and phases of the project. Indicate these by placing them in a chronological order and the specific amount of time required to complete them. You should strive for a clear set of steps in a sequential arrangement. Is the description of these steps consistent with other materials discussed in other sections of the proposal? For example, is there sufficient time set aside for the collection of data? Is there a sufficiency of time allowed for the analysis of data? It may be advisable to consult with others regarding realistic periods of time for the completion of certain tasks. Different tasks require varying lengths of time to complete. The review of literature takes weeks or even months to examine, but it is done in a fairly casual manner, whereas the data collection phase is very often carried out in a very intensive way requiring strict adherence to procedure. The time required to collect data may be only a few days or several months depending on the nature of the problem. The planning of this kind of thing is best done by careful discussion with your advisor or some other knowledgeable person in the field of research methodology.

Experience in the field of research activity suggests that a time table of research activity is probably much too ambitious and will fall way short of the established goals This is especially true of the beginner and the novice. The old hands in the field of research will suggest that a timetable be set up and once it is fixed, the researcher should double the amount of time presumably needed. If there ever was an absolute, this comes close to being one of them. Once the revised time schedule is established, the proposal writer should set his dates of completion for each task. Once this is done, the writer should observe how realistically each study phase can be completed. It is extremely important that the research be carried out according to this calendar of events or adhere to the calendar as closely as possible.

Let it be said that if you are not an experienced researcher. all effort should be made to develop this calendar as realistically as possible. In the face of good or bad advice from other well meaning people, make your timetable, double your time requirements and work like hell to stick to it.

One last comment in regard to scheduling your research work when it involves travel time. When and if your proposed project requires any substantial amount of traveling be extra careful in planning such events. Detail of plan is a most wise posture to take. Traveling takes not only time but money, and wasted travel effort is demoralizing and damages the entire research effort. Again, in this regard as well as all other time scheduling, be conservative and realistic, for once the project is approved and under way, it is extremely difficult to overcome problems of timing and the resulting time binds.

SAMPLING DESIGN AND PROCEDURES

Sampling is a procedure used by scientists in order to generalize about a larger population. Researchers are always worrying about the problem of sampling primarily because of representativeness of that sample But before examining the issue of probability, the proposal writer should begin by defining his unit of study and/or unit of analysis. That is what or who is being studied. The unit of study is better known as a "case" and is statistically referred to as "n" in research reports. The unit of study has one or more common characteristics, that is, all females who are married and have reported physical abuse administered by their husbands. Another example of unit of study might be all social agencies within the city limits of San Juan, Puerto Rico that receive some amount of funding from United Way. All units will have these two characteristics.

Next, the proposal writer should firmly establish the size of the sample and present the rationale for the number of cases selected. The national polling organizations depend on a sample size of around 1200 to 1300 cases and generalize about the population of the entire United States. A sample size of this magniture reduces error from generalizing from a sample to less than one percent. The important issue regarding sample size is not the number of cases included, but how the sample cases were selected. A large number of cases returned from a mailed questionnaire which represents a small return of less than 30 percent is for the most part worthless. A very small sample meticulously selected is far better than a large sample carelessly gathered.

Sampling is important because a great deal of information can be gained from a very limited effort with a well-selected sample. But equally important are two other technical reasons for carefully outlining your proposed sample. First, from the point of view of external validity, it is important so that the researcher may know to whom the results of the study can be generalized. The reviewer or dissertation advisor will want to know the limits and the definition of the population to which you wish to generalize and your exact methods and procedures for selecting a sample from that population. In order to produce a scientific sample, one must draw that sample from the defined population according to some systematic pattern so as to obtain a "probability" sample. Given a probability sample, well known statistical procedures can be readily applied. A defined population has an equal chance of appearing in the sample. Examples of probability samples are the simple random sample, the cluster random sample, the multistage random sample and the stratified random sample. Remember, all forms of probability sampling involve random sampling at some stage in the selection process. The writer should make use of random sampling when the design of his study is survey or experimental where the assignment of cases to both the experimental and control groups should be systematic and random in assignment procedure. A second reason that probability samples are so important is from the point of view of internal validity. Sampling is important because without a probability sample the researcher cannot form a sampling error estimate and thus has no way of judging the precision of statistical results. In many research projects the researcher is simply concerned with the total number of cases being affected by some social problem situation. Rather than selecting a probability sample from a very large population affected by a given problem, the researcher takes a smaller population of the same problem area. The population still needs to be defined; for example, all those cases reported within the city limits of San Juan, Puerto Rico rather than the entire island.

For these reasons, it is important for the proposal writer to describe the particular sampling procedure and the rationale for using that procedure. If one is selecting households from a given neighborhood, he should describe the procedure for selecting the cases. Are you using a sampling method for a mailed questionnaire? Describe the procedures for insuring a reasonably good sample return from a mailed questionnaire. Do not leave your advisor or reviewer guessing as to your intentions. If there is a follow-up sampling process, describe this to your reader. It is important and valuable to make reference to other studies that have used the particular sampling method you hope to employ. This will strengthen your proposal in the eyes of those reviewing your document.

Finally, if there are anticipated difficulties in the sampling phase of your research, it is always best to deal with these difficulties directly. Any experienced reviewer or advisor will spot these problems and confront you with the area of weakness.

DATA COLLECTION INSTRUMENT OR SCHEDULE

This subsection and the following one may be confusing to the reader because they both are concerned with data measurement and data collection. The data collection schedule is a repository and/or a device that contains the instruments that measure the variables necessary to test the research hypotheses and questions. A data collection schedule may very often contain several instruments. It is possible that a data collection schedule contains but one instrument. In this case it may be referred to as a "data collection instrument." Let us illustrate in order to clarify the issue. Age and sex are two variables. The questions posed to respondents, "What is your age? and What is your sex?" are the two instruments attempting to measure the variables of age and sex. The paper that contains the two questions (instruments) is called a data collection schedule. This subsection is concerned with data collection schedules and what the research proposal should say about them. The next subsection is concerned with "instruments" that measure variables.

Before beginning any further discussion, it should be pointed out that when one refers to a "questionnaire," one is referring to a data collection schedule that is completed or filled out by the respondent. A data collection schedule completed by the researcher as observer or interviewer is referred to as a "schedule." It is common to hear the term "questionnaire" in both situations. However, the term questionnaire, when used, still refers to a schedule even when used as a mailed device.

The data collection schedule will more than likely contain more than one instrument. For example, the schedule will include demographic information such as age, sex, education, income, marital status, occupation and family size among other variables. These kinds of variables are relatively easy to measure and present no problem in designing. The schedule will also include the instruments measuring your primary variables. These would be the dependent variable and the independent variable. To illustrate, the study of effectiveness of counseling cancer patients would include counseling and no counseling as the independent variable and "sense of well-being" as the dependent variable. Other variables will be included in your schedule which are referred to as secondary or intervening variables. If the researcher wishes to establish a cause-effect relationship between the independent variable and the dependent, he must always be alert to the intervention of secondary variables. For example, if the researcher has set up a design where counseling is given one group of cancer patients and no counseling is given to a second group of cancer patients with the objective of significantly improving the patients' sense of well-being in the counseled group, all is well. However, if all the counseled patients are female and all the non-counseled patients are male, does this not distort the outcome? What if the counseling group showed statistically significant improvement in the dependent variable of "sense of well-being?" <u>Does this prove counseling caused</u> the improvement? No. The variable of sex may be intervening to significantly affect this outcome. There are a good many variables that may intervene in just this manner. The researcher must control for this kind of unwanted intervention. There are two ways to control for unwanted and unnecessary intervention. One approach is to <u>physically</u> control a variable or set of variables by including them or not including them in the study population. That is, in the problem just mentioned, the researcher could control the variable sex by <u>not including any males in the study at all. This is physically controlling a variable.</u> The second approach is to allow the variable to be included in the project but observe it and analyze the data by determining significance of counseling for female patients as well as non-counseled female patients. Naturally, the same would be true for testing the effect of males as an intervening condition in the study design. The proposal should always include discussion of the control of secondary variables. This kind of discussion clearly illustrates the competence of the proposal writer and begins to point the proper direction for analyzing the data later on when the study is under way.

The different kinds of variables should be listed in a straight-forward manner so that the reader can see very quickly the variables being measured by your instruments. The listing of variables should be accompanied by continual reference to a draft of the data collection schedule that must be attached as an appendix item to the research proposal.

It is wise if each listed variable is identified by level of measurement. If may be necessary to return to a statistics textbook in order to review the data classification chapter. Some writers will recall this system, but others will not. Basically, all data are divided into three categories that actually fall along a continuum from very crude measurement or "nominal" measurements to "ordinal" and then "interval," the most precise level of measurement. Each variable should be identified as to level of measurement by examining the number of categories making up each variable. Again it is suggested that the proposal writer review his statistics text for help in this subject area. This identification of level of measurement will be invaluable later on when the researcher begins the analysis of data. After all, the key to the proper use of statistical analysis is the correct identification of levels of measurement.

When the schedule is being planned, it should be laid out in such a manner as to be attractive and easy to code when the data are finally collected. The schedule should be on good quality paper and printed if cost does not prohibit such luxury. The use of colored paper makes the format so much more inviting and after all, you do want to encourage your respondents to actively complete your instruments. It is also advisable to provide wide margins for each page of the schedule in order that coding the data is convenient and visible.

Finally, it should be said that it is wise to carefully examine the reasons for including each variable in the schedule Do not include a variable if there is no apparent good reason. Very often students will say aaht "it might be nice to include . . . " or "there is still room on the schedule . . . ." These reasons are not sufficient to warrant inclusion of any variable. Include only those variables that you plan to use and analyze.

INSTRUMENTATION, TOOLS FOR MEASURING VARIABLES

Social research, as well as other kinds of research instruments are designed to measure variables. There instruments may be very simple as illustrated in the last subsection regarding the measurement of the variable "age." Age is the variable and the question "What is your age?" is the instrument. This seems obvious and requires little effort to compose such an instrument. Yet there are many other types of instruments that are complicated in their design and construction as well as their scoring procedure.

Detailed discussion of the instruments to be used in a study shows the proposal reviewer that the writer has a sophisticated appreciation for the detail of research methodology. The proposal must reflect this quality. The researcher must design or select from previous studies an instrument or set of instruments for measuring each variable included in the data collection schedule. This process is also known as operationally defining variables. The researcher is trying to determine if the definition through operationalizing the measurement of a variable validly measures that variable. Most important in this regard is the step between conceptualization of a variable and its practical measurement. Is the measurement true to the theoretical meaning embodied in the variable as a concept? The question is a difficult one to answer and other text material on theory and measurement might be helpful. One of the best and most practical approaches to handling this problem is the pretest. Always discuss in your proposal the extent of validity and reliability as shown by any pretesting of your variables. Pretesting is the simplest method to strengthen the meaning of your measurements and their conceptual intent.

For most researchers there are two choices available in regard to instrument design. One is to borrow the necessary tools from other researchers. The second choice is to design your own tools as they are needed. There are many well-designed instruments available and they should be used if they fit your problem.

Too often students will give up the search and fall back on their own skills to design instruments. The search may lead you back to your literature where much discussion was focused on measuring variables. It is wise and economical to use instruments that have already been designed. For one thing, these instruments have probably been tested for reliability and validity, and that needs only to be mentioned in your methodology section of your proposal. Most demographic variables have their validity and reliability based on use and need not be tested except in a pretest operation. It is likely that items from multiple statement scales can be used in your schedule. Many scales have subsections that measure single dimensions that can be lifted out of the original scale and placed in your own data collection schedule. It goes without further mention that all authors of scales or other instruments should be given full credit for their work.

The format of several instruments to be inlcuded in your schedule should follow a logic so that your respondent does not become confused by a jumble of questions and items that make little or no sense to him. For example, some instruments are single dimensional such as the demographic variables mentioned earlier. These may be grouped together while the multiple statement scales may be set off one from another in subsections. This gives proper attention to each instrument or scale. Most collection schedules have some open-ended items. This kind of instrument is valuable for a number of reasons, for it gives the respondent the opportunity to freely express a point of view. Such items should be placed at the very end of the schedule for it is an excellent way for a respondent to conclude his responses to your schedule and blow off some strong feelings.

The range of different kinds of instruments is very great and all are available for your use to measure variables; that is a schedule need not be made up of only one type of instrument. The range of tools is for your use. Among the list of different instruments are the following: scales, ratings, rankings, information check lists, indices, tests of knowledge, questions, open-ended questions, direct observation, tape recordings, life histories, preference tests, and hand-written journals.

VALIDITY AND RELIABILITY

In preparing the research proposal, the confidence one can place in the accuracy of the instruments used goes a long way toward winning acceptance for your proposal. The issues of validity and reliability are the twin pillars that prove research to be only mediocre or outstanding. It is highly recommended that whenever the methods used in research are tried and tested, this fact should be documented, for it greatly increases the strength of your proposal and eventually your research findings.

What do we mean by validity and reliability? Most students of research methodology and statistics are well-informed of the issues involved. If this is not the case, it is suggested that a review of validity and reliability be made. In the meantime a brief reminder of their meanings may be helpful. Validity is concerned with the truth of a measure, that is, does this variable measure what it is supposed to measure? For example, does a clock measure time? Does a speedometer measure how fast you are moving? Are we measuring time and speed or are we measuring something we think is time and speed? Does the instrument measure what it claims to measure? These are hard questions with only vague answers.

Reliability is somewhat more readily understood. Reliability of an instrument is concerned with the consistence of its application. A clock may well be a measure of time but is it a consistent measure of time? If an instrument consistently measures time incorrectly, one is unable to use the instrument. If we know that the clock is always off by say, five minutes, then it is not a valid instrument but it is reliable. The difficulty with testing instruments for these methodological dimensions only goes to underscore the strength of your instruments when validity and reliability are present. Then, too, an instrument may have reliability and not validity or the reverse condition. From an operational point of view, it is probably best if your instrument has at least demonstrated reliability. For an instrument to have some reliability, it automatically has a small amount of validity built into it. Finally, it needs to be pointed out that most demographic data and other observable behavior has what is called "face" validity. This consists of well-defined understanding of what, let us say, age means. The culture literally demands that its citizens know and measure such variables as age, sex, education, income, and a whole host of behaviors necessary in order to negotiate everyday life.

PRETESTING THE DATA COLLECTION SCHEDULE

The pretest is also sometimes referred to as a "pilot test." Even if a data collection schedule has valid and reliable instruments, it is always wise to plan to submit your schedule to some kind of pretest. A pretest is submitting the instruments to a very small group of respondents who should be encouraged to be critical of the schedule and its instruments. This kind of pretest may consist of only five or six subjects. The value of this procedure can only be realized after submitting a set of instruments to a study population and finding errors and embarrassing omissions. A simple pretest will quickly assess for the researcher errors that can be quickly corrected. The comments of a pretest group are sometimes invaluable in showing insight that only the researcher would overlook because he is much too close to his work. For these reasons, he should include a pretest or "test run" before the actual serious data collection gets under way. It need not be indicated in the proposal, but on some occasions the cases used in the pretest can also be included as part of the actual data to be collected. This is possible when and if the pretest cases can be legitimately included in the sample and there are no serious errors in the instruments as designed.

DEFINITION OF THE MOST IMPORTANT TERMS AND CONCEPTS

Why define terms in the research proposal? Every researcher knows that a clear understanding of terms and concepts is necessary in order to communicate to other scientists and scholars. There must be a common understanding of what is being referred to during the presentation of findings. But the need to define has already been discussed in a previous subsection. That is under the discussion of the data collection schedule and instrumentation, variables were listed and measured. The process of describing and measuring variables is in fact a process of defining terms and concepts. For example, if the concept "mastery over life" were used as a measure of control, the definition of this concept would consist of the individual items making up the scale that measures "mastery over life." Measuring a variable is synonymous with defining that variable.

During the development of your review of literature, there will be a great deal of reference made to technical terms and concepts. The understanding of these items is most important to the reviewer or advisor in order that he quickly grasp the full impact of your problem and your particular theoretical approach to it. It is for this reason that technical terms be clearly defined in this section of the proposal. It should be remembered that once the research has been completed and the final document is available to any and all eyes, the non-expert and the non-specialist may find good reason to ready your work. This audience will need to have the technical terms defined for them in order that a full appreciation of your work can be experienced. Moreover, the greater the depth of the proposal writer's involvement with his work, the less sensitive he is to the clarity of his own writing. He gets lost in his own fascination with the problem and fails to see that what is common and obvious to him is foreign and obscure to others. This does not mean that every term or concept should be defined in this subsection. You must be selective and this may require that a second reader can more objectively help make the judgment as to what should be defined here and what need not be defined in this section.

ADMINISTRATION OF THE DATA COLLECTION SCHEDULE

Other subsections have dealt with the data collection schedule and its design. Following that, a discussion on instrumentation was presented. This subsection is primarily concerned with the actual procedures for the collection of data. The proposal should reflect rather clearly how the administration of the collection schedule should proceed because this is the most critical period in the entire research process including the preparation of the research proposal. It is critical because the time factor is determined by real respondents who are not necessarily interested in whether you finish your project or not. In one sense, all the stages of planning and carrying out the project have been within the direct control of the researcher. This is not so when the collection of data is under way. The research is especially vulnerable if the data are collected from personal interviews. Only well-trained interviewers can give the researcher any reassurance that the process will be accurately and correctly done within the time limits set forth in the proposal's calendar of events. Some research which relies on files as the source of data greatly reduces the potential anxiety of the researcher because such data can be more systematically organized for collection. If the data are to be collected from respondents by interview, it would be advisable to give the interviewer some training before sending them out to get your data. The reviewer or research advisor will want to know the specifics of your plans for the collection of data and that will include explicit statements about the field controls you will employ. In regard to the use of field interviewers, the social and psychological aspects of studies are all too often ignored. For example, the use of white interviewers in a black community or the casual interview manner used in gathering data on the sensitive subject of child or wife abuse will probably lead to a distortion of the information gathered. In both examples the social dynamics of the data collection situation, if ignored, may damage the study's validity. Respondents are normally and under most circumstances helpful and honestly responsive and that is to your best advaatage in producing accurate and valid information. It is up to the researcher not to damage that trust but to build on it. The respondent is extremely important to the project and therefore great care must be taken to "protect" the respondent from unnecessary interruption and disturbance. You must remember that the respondent is doing you a favor and not the other way around. In community surveys a specific set of field instructions should be given to each interviewer before data are gathered. One of these instructions should speak to the need to not disrupt the respondent or draw unnecessary attention to the respondent and his normal environment. Most researchers are sensitive to and must guard against producing the "Hawthorne Effect," that is, the effect that the very doing of a study has upon the group involved. Some populations have been overstudied, such as groups of delinquents and clients of social agencies. Before leaving the issue of unplanned for effects, the proposal writer should make special effort to deal with negative reactions that are likely to be involved with controversial research subject matter. Studies done dealing with incest, child abuse, wife abuse, sexual matters and criminal behavior to name but a few sensitive topical areas, can lead to difficulty in the data collection phase. You must try to anticipate these kinds of situations and to prevent problems before they start. It goes without further mention that whatever the source of data and the method of its collection, always respect those agents or persons that provide access to the information.

There are numerous methods of acquiring data and the proposal writer should be acquainted with most of them either through long experience or review of basic general methodology textbook material. This method should be spelled out carefully in the proposal. There are several methods that are common in data collection and they are: personal interview which yields some of the most reliable information, telephone interview, group response where a great deal of data can be gathered at one time if the respondents are located in one place as a group for some reason, records and files, direct observation and mailed questionnaires. The last method has been used extensively and yields an enormous amount of good information; however, one should be familiar with the pitfalls of the mailed schedule. It is highly recommended that text reading on the subject be consulted if the researcher is inexperienced in the use of the method. Mailed questionnaires are inexpensive but yield a low return in terms of mail-back from respondents. It is wise to plan this kind of operation with a great deal of care in order not to be disappointed in the yield rate and therefore potentially damage your study validity.

Finally, a few thoughtful words to remind the research prosooal writer that at the bottom of all this effort is the individual who records the data and/or the respondent who must give you the information in writing or verbally. Remember, data are only as good as the original information sources; therefore, it is the researcher's responsibility to frame and design the collection instruments in such a way as to help the respondent quickly and easily measure in his mind the information the researchers wants and needs

DATA PROCESSING PROCEDURES

Many research proposals include little or nothing about the data processing aspects of doing a piece of research. Again, the lack of any comment suggests to the proposal reviewer that no thought has been given to this aspect of the research process or that the researcher is simply unaware of its importance to the project. If the research design is case study or historical, then the processing of data is irrelevant and no further thought need be given to it. However, if the study involves quantitative analysis of data, then some discussion is in order.

What is meant by data processing? Data processing is concerned with the transfer of collected data to a coded form that is entered onto a data processing instrument which in turn is manipulated in such a way as to produce statistical and/or numerically arranged data. There are several methods including marginal punch cards, simple hand sort-count and record from the data collection schedule, and the eighty column punch card commonly associated with computer data analysis. More and more research on and off the college campus is being done with the assistance of computer equipment. The capacity of this technology is so superior to the old manual methods of sort-count and record that there is no comparison in terms of efficiency and accuracy. Computer analysis provides the researcher with the capacity to manipulate data in many different ways and make possible highly sophisticated and precise understanding of data collected. It should be remembered that since great effort has been expended on the research project up to this point, it certainly deserves careful and generous treatment when it comes to the analysis of data.

There are computer centers on almost every university campus and consultants are available to give you assistance in preparing your data for processing and analysis. It is recommended in the planning of the data collection schedule that coding of the variables should be worked out. That is, the writer should return to his list of variables under the subsection "Data Collection Schedule." Each variable should be assigned categorieswhich can in turn be assigned numerical values, for example, female -1 and male -2 or strongly agree -1, agree -2, undecided -3, disagree -4, and strongly disagree -5. This arrangement of coded variables by category is referred to as "Coding Instructions." The coding instructions are necessary if the data are to be punched into cards and processed by computer equipment. Again, the proposal should at least include a coding system for all variables categories if the researcher plans to use computer services. The coding of categories can be done on the margins of the attached instruments or listed separately as an attachment to the proposal.

PROCEDURES OF DATA ANALYSIS

The research design subsection of the proposal focuses attention on the basic contrasts and comparisons to be made in order to test the major and minor questions and hypotheses. The "Procedures of Data Analysis" subsection of the proposal makes somewhat more explicit the technical procedures necessary to carry out the charge expressed in the design subsection.

The proposal should show what groups are to be compared and what statistical tests and measures will be used to determine statistical significance. In the situation of the casestudy or historical designs, the researcher will want to indicate the specific use of non-statistical as well as statistical techniques. Non-statistical techniques will include the use of photographs, maps, drawings and illustrations. Statistical technique will include the use of statistical tables, frequency counts, and percentages for summarizing data and making simple comparisons possible. If the proposal writer is skilled in the use of bivariate and multivariate analysis (which the computer equipment can easily perform), then these statistical tests should be mentioned in this subsection of the proposal. Some of the more common data analysis designs would include chi square analysis, product moment correlation coefficiency, and "t" test, analysis of variance and Mann-Whitney u analysis.

SPECIAL TECHNIQUES

It has been mentioned earlier that each project will be unique and this writer respects that character of your work. It is likely that the uniqueness of your work is sufficient to warrant the preparation of a special section and eventually a special chapter in the final research document to describe this uniqueness. For example, for those researchers who find the need to develop and construct a special scale or instrument, the procedures involved should be outlined in a special section of the proposal. This development of an instrument is valuable not only to the researcher, but also the potential users who read your final document. Another example of a special section is the extended history. When a little known area is being investigated, the researcher may find it necessary to inform his reader of the historical background to the problem. He should prepare a detailed outline of this section to be included in the proposal. The complicated construction of equipment necessary to test and measure or otherwise use in a project might warrant detailed description in the final document. This, too, should be outlined in the proposal. Do not feel reluctant to make the effort to include special mention of unique features of your research, for this will almost always be viewed as competency on the part of the proposal writer by reviewers and academic advisors.

PROTECTION OF HUMAN SUBJECTS

Many of the social and political changes of the 1960's and 70's have meant increasing concern and consideration for the rights of individuals heretofore ignored by those with power and prestige. This movement has led to the passage of legislation that attempts to guarantee the equal treatment of individuals under specified circumstances. Much of this legislation may be described as civil rights and the guarantees of civil liberties. The university is no exception to this influence and why should it be? Research on or off the campus is impacting on all kinds of people from medical research in university hospitals to demonstration projects in urban neighborhoods and rural communities. Human beings are very often the subject of considerable investigation and legislation now exists to protect such individuals from obvious or subtle and sometimes insidious abuse.

66

Universities now require that research projects which make use, in any way, of human beings must provide written statements that describe the involvement of the human subjects in the research process. The researcher is asked to attempt to guarantee that the subject will be protected from physical or psychological harm. This is done primarily by informing the subjects of their right to volunteer or not to volunteer for participation in the research. If the rights of respondents or their records are to be involved in a research effort, provisions should be made to insure confidentiality. If a patient or client's records from an agency in the community are to be used, evidence of that agency's approval and cooperation should be indicated in the research proposal. Many institutions are formulating guidelines to insure the protection of the rights of persons housed by that institution. The researcher needs only to request a copy of these guidelines in order to achieve proper authority to begin his research with individuals maintained by that institution.

What is needed are reassurances that your research will respect the rights of those human beings participating in the study. The proposal should discuss this aspect and quiet the worries of the reviewer or academic advisor. Most universities have some review committee that requires a statement from the researcher that adequate protection will be guaranteed for all respondents.

REPORT FORMAT OUTLINE

The research proposal is nearing completion and only the list of references and the data collection schedule remain to be attached to the document. Many experienced researchers, when writing a proposal for a new project, can quite easily anticipate the form and character of the final chapters of the research report long before the research actually begins. Very often this will include one or more "findings" chapters and a "summary, conclusions, and recommendations" chapter. For research using designs other than quantitative-statistical methods, the outline of chapters is somewhat different and requires an examination of the data for logical clusterings around topical areas. Chapter titles and subheadings are then assigned appropriately. It is recommended that an outline of the final research report format be placed at the very end of the research proposal. This is not absolutely necessary but it would stretch your imagination and further clarify the entire research process from beginning to end. In laying out the report format, and especially those last chapters with subheadings, the hypotheses major and minor will be visualized as data-producing devices that are carried out to the final stage of testing for acceptance or rejection. Again, there is no absolute need to outline the final report and many proposal writers may lack the research experienced to do so easily, but for the old hand, the task is relatively simple.

ATTACHMENTS

The list of references should be placed at the conclusion of the written proposal document. Kate L. Turabian (1973) is an excellent standard reference for the preparation and use of footnotes and bibliographic listings. There are numerous methods for footnoting and any one of them is available to complement your own style and preference. After selecting a style, be sure to be consistent with the use of it. A bibliography may be included at the very end of the proposal. This should include all footnote references organized into categories such as books, journal articles, newspaper references, unpublished speeches, interviews and unpublished manuscripts and papers. Be sure to give credit for interviews, for this too, should be valued by a grateful researcher. When the research has been completed and the report is finished, you may wish to add other reference material gathered during the final writing of the report.

The data collection schedule will be attached following the footnote reference list. This should be carefully typed or printed in the form that you anticipate using when the collection of data beigns. Earlier some mention was made of coding the categories to each variable in the collection schedule. This coding process can be carried out directly on the attached draft of the schedule. If the coding process tends to clutter the data schedule and detract from its normal appearance, the coding can be done on separate sheets listing each variable and the coded categories. This listing can be attached immediately following the schedule.

FINAL TASKS AFTER THE FIRST DRAFT OF THE

RESEARCH PROPOSAL IS FINISHED

When a proposal has been completed, students sometimes wonder if the proposal is long enough to suit the advisor. If the proposal is prepared for grant competition, contracted research as well as the thesis or dissertation, the same question may be asked. For experienced researchers, there is no thought of proper length unless there are guidelines that specify an appropriate length. Many doctoral dissertation proposals will be as long as 60 or more pages typed and double spaced. This is not excessive if all attachments are included and a comprehensive review of literature is included. Some thesis proposals will be as short as 20 pages typed and double spaced. There is no answer to the question of length except to say "long enough to say what needs to be said." No one is ever going to tell you that a proposal is too long or too short. Chances are, less criticism is likely if it is very long rather than very short. The criticism will probably be aimed at what is not covered or <u>areas that are not adequately covered</u>. Different reviewers will look more intently for different things. Some reviewers will want more depth to your review of literature, while others will want further elaboration on aspects of methodology. If you can easily ascertain the preferences of your reader, then do so, and have them reflected in the proposal writing process. There is one precaution that needs repeating but once and that is do not fill your proposal with <u>filler</u> just to take up page space. This practice only tends to irritate the reviewer rather than appeal to his intellectual curiousity. Experienced researchers are wise to all the tricks used to camouflage a poorly prepared document, so do not encourage criticism. Develop skill and apply it to the task at hand.

THINGS YOU SHOULD REMEMBER TO DO

The proposal has been finished but not submitted for review and/or approval. If there are any second thoughts about the value of this project, it is best to seriously re-think the whole thing now. The experienced researcher will have no reservations after having gone this far, but this is not true of the inexperienced student. Upon completion of this much work on the proposal, some students suddenly become reluctant to carry the project any further. Some of this apparent trepidation is due to overwhelming self criticism of the proposal. The writer will simply feel it is too much to undertake at this time and will quickly begin to look for another less complicated project. The writer may very legitimately find the project is too difficult to carry out without a great deal of assistance from others. Obviously, it suggests that consultation with knowledgeable persons is not only a good idea but essential. Consultation should begin immediately after the idea's inception and should continue on a regular basis until the final proposal draft is completed. It is hoped if there is reservation about the project that such reservation will diminish and disappear with continual progress on the proposal.

When the first completed draft of the proposal is ready for editing, the writer should begin to locate a knowledgeable person for the purposes of critiquing your work. It is certainly acceptable to have one of your friends read your material, but experience indicates that friends are wonderful companions, but make poor research proposal critics. Find someone who is more distant or takes a professional view of such matters. Such persons will be much more objective and conscientious critics and that is exactly what you are looking for at this time. If such a critic appears to be too severe with your work, you can always ignore as much of his criticism as you so wish. But experienced researchers prefer a severe critic to one that is passive and reluctant to risk injury to your ego. Take all the criticism you can get and make the best possible use of it. Good critics may be difficult to find, and it might be necessary to pay a consultant a fee to attract the services of a good critic. But you are highly committed to this project and have devoted many hours of work to its present level of completion so don't stop now. The project deserves the very best care and attention.

During the process of editing and using critical consultation, your first draft copy could disappear. Stranger things have been known to happen. For this reason among others, have five or six copies reproduced while retaining two or three copies at all times. At this point you may have a friend who is sufficiently interested in your proposal to take a copy and study it. This is flattering and possibly useful to you, but the point is that copies do tend to disappear and extra drafts need to be available.

THINGS YOU SHOULD REMEMBER NOT TO DO

When the first complete draft is finished, there are a number of things you should not do. Inexperience does not serve the novice researcher well in these situations. First, do not make the mistake of thinking this is just another "paper" among many that have to be completed within a required time frame. It is not just another paper! Do not consider this document unimportant. Second, there is the tendency to hasten all those final writing chores, and this is a mistake. For example, typing your draft with the same old typing ribbon that has been used for the last two years is wrong. Don't do it! Borrow some money and buy a new ribbon. Third, do not leave your proposal at a friend's house. On occasion, students and others have been known to have carried their only proposal copy with them to visit friends, relatives, and others and left the only draft behind or worse yet, on a plane. Airline companies have not been known to show much gratitude when suddenly becoming the benefactor of a research proposal. Fourth, another common mistake made by the inexperienced is the use of cheap and inexpensive materials. Just because you may have lots of cheap paper left by a previous tenant, don't use it. Buy the best quality paper that can be found. Even if several drafts and revisions are necessary, bear the expense. Remember, this is not just another term paper. Finally, it is highly recommended that the proposal writer locate a typist who is a professional. If you are not a proficient typist, do not type your own work. Hire a competent typist to do it for you.

THINGS TO DO WITH THE PROPOSAL WHEN THE RESEARCH IS COMPLETED

Let us assume that your proposal has been accepted and the research process has been followed through the data collection and processing phases. It is obvious that reference to the proposal has been casual if not intense at particular times. By this point into the research, the steps and stages have become familiar to you and use of the proposal declines as work on the project proceeds. The question is of what value is the proposal at this stage of events? The proposal remains valuable for one basic reason. All of the material that was written into the proposal is certainly a part of the overall project. When the analysis of data is under way, the writer can turn his thoughts to shaping the first three chapters of the research report. It is not necessary to wait until the data are completely processed or analyzed before the report wirting phase can begin.

First, begin by taking a spare copy of the proposal and removing each section for separate use and examination. Next, reread the introduction with a view of changing it to "Introduction" Chapter 1 of the report. It will be necessary to change tenses. It will also be necessary to remove those statements, questions, and hypotheses that no longer fit with the reality of the actual research. Move to the second section, "Review of Literature." Follow the same procedure as you did in the first section. Start thinking and reading as if it were the second chapter of your final report. During the research work you will have undoubtedly discovered additional literature relevant to the project. In this event, this new material should be added and integrated into the literature chapter. Again, the rewriting task will require changing tenses. Move to the methodology section and continue the process of rereading, changing tenses, adding material and removing inappropriate parts. No researcher is so wise that all plans work perfectly. The methodology chapter must reflect the actual facts of the research experience. If a special section has been written about the unique aspects of "interviewer training," and has been placed under the subsection "Special Techniques" of the research proposal, the writer may want to pull this out of the methodology section and create an entirely new chapter in the research report.

With relatively little effort, the writer has converted the research proposal into four chapters of the final report, Chapter 1. INTRODUCTION; Chapter 2 REVIEW OF LITERATURE; Chapter 3. METHODOLOGY; Chapter 4, INTERVIEWER TRAINING. At this point, the writer is ready to organize the "Findings" chapter around the major research questions and hypotheses.

This monograph has been written primarily for the thesis or dissertation student. The applicability of these proposal guidelines goes far beyond the academic audience, however. There is no reason why these guidelines cannot be applied to any research problem. Many researchers doing consultant work may find the guidelines useful as a reference. Many others in professional evaluation work, especially in the human services, can readily make use of the guidelines as a referral source. Much consultant and contract research work does not specifically call for competing for grant moneys, but does require careful preparation of proposals as a part of their professional activity. For those who are drawn to the competition of grantsmanship, the development of skill in this exciting enterprise is absolutely essential for any reasonable amount of success. Basic to this development of skill is a sound research and statistics background with a reasonably sophisticated use of computer technology. Many who are in the process of acquiring these technical skills may wish to try their hand at grantsmanship. This portion of the monograph is desinged for that kind of beginning and promising grantsman (grantsperson).

Much of the material written about proposal writing is devoted and dedicated to helping researchers win money grants. Readers are encouraged to go to their local public library or favorite books and select one of the several treatises on the subject. But for now, the following notes should inform and provide the background for the library or bookstore trip.

This writer has won a few and lost a few grants, but the experience has been interesting and mostly encouraging. If you have the urge to try your hand at a grant, do so! Small grants are obviously easier to win than large ones. Large ones are in the range of over $10,000 and small ones would be something less than this sum. If you are in the $100,000 frame of mind, don't read any further. This writer has contributed directly to two such grants, one won and one lost. At this level of grantsmanship, one must join a team of experts to write a winning proposal. However, this writer's experience with small grants and grantsmanship leads him to unequivocally say they are an awful lot of fun and provide one with the clear sense of contributing to one's professional field. But again, it bears repeating that you will win a few and lose a few.

ADAPTING THE PROPOSAL FOR GRANT COMPETITION

The guidelines have focused attention and dealt with preparing proposals primarily for theses and dissertations. The following considerations, when applied to the guidelines, can easily begin to convert the thesis or dissertation into a suitable proposal for grant competition. As mentioned earlier, there are numerous publications that have been written expressly for grant proposal writing. An excellent source for this purpose is Krathwohl's (1965) book How To Prepare a Research Proposal and Mary Hall's (1971) book, Developing Skills in Proposal Writing.

Let us begin with the following suggestions for adapting your proposal for grant competiton. Begin with a review of your proposal as prepared, using the proposal outline and the accompanying guidelines. The research proposal is the only communications device by which the worth of the project can be judged. Make certain that it spells out exactly what is intended to be accomplished by the proposal writer. It should convey to the reviewer a thorough understanding of the literature and be written in such a manner that the means used to evaluate the proposal stands out clearly and succinctly. The proposal should be written in direct language. Make certain that ideas are clearly delineated and most of all, avoid the use of professional jargon. Write the proposal in terms intelligible to someone who is generally sophisticated but who is not well-informed in the area of the problem. This is especially important for the abstract which accompanies the proposal. Try to write the abstract so that a well-informed person can understand what is proposed (Veri, 1968).

Remember, the way to get started in this business is to start small and don't get in over your head. Next, find out in exact terms what the grantor organization is looking for in the way of type of field and project. Develop a very brief abstract to be no longer than one single page describing the project. Finally, make use of other professionals in your field who have successfully won grants. This last point is a must for your first or second try at grantsmanship.

PROCEDURES OF THE GRANT GIVING ORGANIZATION

The deadlines for submission of proposals vary considerably. Federal agencies are more lenient that in the past. Most foundations set deadlines but adjustments can be made because there is usually a series of deadlines marking off different phases of the application process. If one deadline is not met, the next one will do just fine. All grant giving organizations have available procedure forms along with their application material. These pamphlets and forms give specific information regarding deadlines.

It would be difficult to describe in any detail the procedures by which a research proposal is accepted or rejected since each granting agency has its own system for processing proposals. In general, a proposal goes through the following steps regardless of the type of grant giving organization. The proposal is reproduced in sufficient quantities and is received by the granting organization. It is then sent to the appropriate office within the organization for screening. The proposal is assigned a project number and project officer. It may be distributed to members of the review committee. Another possible review alternative is having copies of the proposal routed to a select body of outside consultants who read and review the document. Whatever the makeup of the review team, they will examine the document for: a) problem significance, b) general design or plan, c) adequacy of resources, and d) economic efficiency. The review consultants then rate the proposal according to some kind of standardized scale.

PREPARING THE PROPOSAL ABSTRACT

It is absolutely necessary to prepare a proposal abstract. The reviewers will start with this kind of statement. The abstract can serve as a source of discussion if and when an interview is granted. If there are several consultants involved, the abstract can serve as an easy reference point for their discussion of the project and its strengths and weaknesses.

The abstract will normally appear at the beginning of the proposal. But it should be written after the proposal has been completely developed and finalized. The abstract usually includes the major objectives of the proposal and the procedures. It should not exceed one or two pages. It should preferably be less than one page. The length of the abstract is usually specified in the grant organization's application guidelines. The abstract usually serves a number of purposes. The review team member usually reads it first to gain a perspective on the study. Next, review team members use it to remind themselves of the nature of the study when the project comes up for discussion. It will usually be the only part of the proposal that is read by those reviewing a team's recommendation. With these several uses, it is clear that the abstract should (1) be prepared with care, (2) paraphrase the objectives and procedures using broad but accurate descriptors and keeping parts in proper perspective with appropriate emphasis, and (3) employ the key ideas and terms used in the body of the material so as to prepare the reader for them.

USING CONSULTANTS

Those proposal writers just beginning a grantsmanship career have little or no reputation as a resource in the arduous battle for grants. Building a reputation is extremely difficult unless you have a famous name coming from a famous relative. For ordinary souls which most of us are, finding and using a reputation is a major task. To attract attention to your project, it is best to attach a reputable research name and talent to your proposal. It is regrettable that so many splendid projects are never carried out because there are no "big named authorities" associated with them. Those who have a noteworthy reputation are the ones who usually get the best grants and the rest are left with the small potatoes. The proposal writer who can show a long history of successful work in the area, in an institutional setting well equipped to handle such problems, is way ahead of his competition. Your own reputation and that of your institution or organization are also important factors. Put your best foot forward. Prepare a carefully detailed resume of your own accomplishments. Begin to look around and seek out assistance from people at your organization or institution and in your local area who have successfully received funds. Don't operate in a vacuum. Build on the experience of others. Seek consultant help from someone who knows the agency to which you are addressing your request, and who knows the current thinking in that agency. Don't overlook the fact that the best consultants are agency personnel. A trip to Washington with a preliminary draft for an informal conversation can be very helpful in "selling" your projects. Seek the assistance of budget experts at your institution. This will include such people as the business manager, the campus research foundation and others who have overall responsibility for representing the institution for funded projects.

Inasmuch as most proposals benefit from consultant help, it has become almost impossible to choose from among them on the basis of sheer competence or form of the proposal. All proposals are slickly done. Hence, decisions are more and more made on the basis of who the proposal writer is and what institution he represents. An outstanding person can get support for even a bizarre proposal, but a relatively unknown person should stick to studies which fit the proposal format reasonably well.

THE USE OF OTHER PERSONNEL

Almost every project with a budget over $2000 may very well require the services of more than the principal investigator. There are interviewers, data analysis experts, and research assistants to be employed by the project. These and all other consultants should be listed by name, title and a brief statement of relevant experience. If the person has any special and unique qualifications, that should be indicated too. Be sure to include the research projects and publications of each person, especially the consultants. A novice researcher can very often increase his chances for winning a grant if one or more well-established researchers can be signed up for your project. You obviously must secure the names of these individuals long before the project is awarded a grant and this may not be so easy to do. Some of these persons will give tentative approval to you to use their names. But the use of active consulting participation does give the reviewer or review team assurance that the probability of sponsoring a successful project is increased. Finally, something must be said for the problem of enlisting personnel and yet not hiring them. In the preparations of a research proposal which includes a large or small number of persons to be employed, it is highly unlikely that any of these persons will be willing to commit themselves to a position to begin at some unspecified time in the future on a project that might not be funded at all. Do not concern yourself with this seemingly intractable problem. You need not expect potential project staff people to commit themselves to a non-existent project. All you really need from them is a tentative agreement to participate in the project. If and when the project is funded, these commitments need not be honored. Other replacement staff persons can be sought out and lined up when the project gets under way.

BUDGET CONSIDERATIONS

Theses and dissertations, like any other kind of research involve time and cost (time is money). When an investigator submits a research proposal for consideration as a candidate in competition for a research grant, such proposals are accompanied by an itemized statement of anticipated costs. Even when an investigator finances his own research, it is very sensible to prepare a budget of time and other costs involved. When expenses are itemized, feasibility of the project is more clearly understood. Is the budget realistic as indicated by previous contracts or grants for similar work from the same sponsor? Are unusually expensive parts of the budget itemized and justified? Does the work schedule reflect budget consideration? Has the work schedule been specified clearly, and is it realistic in terms of time and money? Is there too much dependence on "consultants"? Is there too little planned for interviewers?

The budget is an operational statement in monetary terms. A carefully thought out project translates easily into specific amounts. Budget preparation is a good test of how carefully one has thought through the details of the procedure.

It is rarely true that the proposal is the last chance at budget specification. Cuts may be made or recommended in the budget as a concession for proposal approval.

Interestingly enough, the budget is the section that the beginner fears the most, but the experienced researcher fears the least. Discovering a good research idea and translating it into a means for its investigation is the hard work. The rest is easy if one can find someone who knows the prices of such things as secretaries, pocket calculators or whatever is needed. It also relieves a little of the anxiety to remember that the budget submitted is rarely the final one. It is usually subject to negotiation after the decision to support the project is made. The total may go up or down under negotiation. The granting organization wants the researcher to have enough funds to complete the project properly as much as the researcher himself does. In addition, amendments to the project can usually be made if adequate reason is given and funds are available. There usually are limits on the size of what is added without the submission of a new proposal. It is well to know the limits in advance but it is usually small relative to the average size of grants. That is, what can be realistically added is relatively small, in the range of ten or fifteen percent.

As an operational statement in money terms, all the budgetary provisions should have a counterpart in the project description. Developing the budget is an excellent test of how operationally the project has been described. A clearly described project and precise time schedule will be easily translated into budgetary terms. A vague one will be translated only with elaborate guess work. If much of this occurs, re-examine the proposal write-up; it may need a more careful re-writing.

You should budget for the costs of administering the research project. This would mean that it is perfectly permissible to include funds for the salary of the investigators (you) so that they may be free to do the research. Strive to account for all costs. For example, a social service agency might allow an experiment on different practice models. Even though the agency pays the workers who try out the different practice models, account for the cost of this essential part of the research project. Budget it as a contribution of the agency, and specify the amount of money. Also, assume that the project will be directed by a competent researcher other than yourself and budget for hsi salary. The beginning researcher almost always underestimates the cost of a proposed research project. He seldom accounts for such costs as the time needed for pre-testing instruments or the time involved in writing a proposal which has the potential for making a significant contribution to knowledge. A carefully executed research project included a well written final report which is always far more time consuming than is estimated by beginning researchers. As for the time schedule, it is easy to underestimate the costs of complete data collection and the final report preparation. Allow enough in these categories. If necessary, tend toward over-budgeting and you will probably end up with adequate funds in this area. Similarly, already committed requirements on equipment need to be studied to determine whether special budgetary provisions for rental or purchase of some additions are desirable. Be sure to check the budgetary restrictions on equipment. In this regard, the researcher should carefully itemize costs and/or use of needed facilities such as computer time, automobile use, hand calculators and special equipment.

Too often the beginning researcher will let this section go until the very last moment and hastily record rough estimates. Do not jot down figures which have little basis in fact. The researcher should be aware that should the project be approved, he may be asked to give a rationale for various items in the budget. The extent of this probing varies with the sponsor, so it is best to be prepared.

Finally, has someone who knows the costs of relevant items and salaries checked your work? It is absolutely essential that a knowledgeable person with budget experience examine your proposal section on budget.

THE REVIEW PROCESS

What is the process through which the proposal will pass on its way to acceptance or rejection? Have you considered the implications of the review procedure by which the proposal will be evaluated? You should try to learn as much as possible about the review process even before the first draft of the proposal is finished. Knowledge of the review procedure will identify what sections of the proposal will be given the greatest amount of attention and careful scrutiny. If this is known, then precise wording or elaboration can be applied to those sections.

Sometimes knowledge of the members of the review team will suggest particular concerns and personal biases. You can certainly play to those interests and biases. There is absolutely nothing wrong with anticipating the preferences of review team members. They are human too. They have likes and dislikes which, if you know, can serve your interest and the interests of your project. This is certainly true of approval committees for thesis and dissertation proposals. The academic setting reflects interest and biases of individuals and it is in your best interest to take these into account when presenting your proposal for their review.

Grant giving organizations tend to be reluctant to reveal the professional and specialist interests of their review teams. It is best to design your proposal to meet the interests of both specialist and non-specialist. For the non-specialist, make sure that professional jargon is explained and/or defined. For the specialists who will probably be on the team, make sure that the literature is carefully reviewed and thereby show your knowledge and competence of the field of study in which your research problem emanates. Almost invariably the specialist or expert will focus on that section of the proposal which he feels most competent to criticize. But it is most likely that the review team will be composed of non-specialists and specialists, and you must strive to meet the expectations of both types of readers.

Reviewers are individuals who are experienced in the task of proposal review and evaluation. They frequently have a large volume of different proposals to examine. It is for this reason that the pressured reviewer is given every opportunity to easily and quickly read the critically important parts of the research proposal. A hasty reading means some parts will be overlooked, and only the most highlighted (underlined) material will get the most attention. Ideally, each proposal writer expects that his proposal will be given as much time as necessary to adequately read, comprehend, and evaluate it. This writer has served on review teams and has had every intention of giving each proposal a thorough reading with thoughtful notations made for each. The realities are that under the pressure of time and enornous amounts of materials to read, the reviewer gives way to very hasty review. The experience is universally true of practically all review readers.

Therefore, it is always safe to assume that the proposal might have to be reviewed under time pressures. It is for this reason that the proposal writer follows with care the grant application guidelines for writing the proposal. These grant forms may look casual enough, but follow their instructions and suggestions very carefully and precisely.

SELECTING THE RIGHT FUNDING AGENCY

Is the proposal being sent to the right sponsor? Do you know the interest and purposes of the granting organization? For the best results, it is necessary that you find out as much as possible about the grantor in order to match your proposal to the right grantor. If you do not know the grantor's goals and objectives, you may very well be wasting your time. When a researcher contracts with a sponsor or organization, the purposes and needs of the sponsor are well known. When competing for a grant, this is far less clear. Civic and philanthropic foundations are rarely as stringent in their requirements as state or federal organizations (Krathwohl, 1966). They are more open as to style and time deadlines, but still have fairly clear purposes and objectives for their organization. Federal agencies are more stringent in terms of guidelines, but equally concerned with specific goals and agency objectives. It is best to request specific information from the agency or organization whose purpose is identical with your proposal study. If you can acquire this information through a personal interview or contact, by all means do so. Given this kind of information , you then know the direction for developing your proposal. Some grantors may have geographical qualifications, restricting requests for grant applications to a given city, or state or regional district. Almost every sponsoring agency may want to fund a wide variety of projects but in reality they can support only a limited number of projects which they feel will have a significant impact on a particular field. More often a funding agency will concentrate its resources in a few areas. This kind of approach is established by the agency's board. All federal agencies are limited in the kinds of research they can fund either by law, which established the program or the agency's interpretation of the policy which is the result of some legally established provision. However, most foundations and governmental funding agencies will supply a list of recently funded research projects. Such information serves as an excellent guide to the agency's interests. As previously suggested, some kind of personal contact with the potential sponsor is the best means for clarifying its policy regarding kinds of research it will fund.

HARD EVIDENCE ON EASY SUCCESS: A FINAL NOTE

The preceding discussion on grantsmanship is based on the experience of this writer as an occasional pursuer of grants with moderate success and a member of a review team which granted funds to projects. The discussion is also reflective of the experience of many others who have been successful at winning grants and have written succinctly on the subject of grants and granstmanship. In order to conclude this discussion, a final reference is made to a piece of research by June Siegel (Siegel, 1977). Her master's thesis was focused on the identification of factors related to successful grantsmanship among social service agencies. Her findings and conclusions, even though focused on foundations, support nearly all that has been discussed in the preceding subsections. Six of her seven hypotheses were supported by strong evidence. The evidence supporting these hypotheses are discussed in the following:

(a)   Significant variables in obtaining foundation grants are: political factors ("who you are and who you know"), knowing foundation staff, prestige of the applicant, knowledge of the funding foundation and the significance of the proposal.

(b)   Proposals should be concise and specific. All sections in the proposal are important and, therefore, only thoroughly thought out; well written documents should be submitted to the funding agency.

(c)   The easiest grants to obtain are one-time only grants and matching grants.

(d)   Actively researching funding agencies means: knowing their donors, assets, staff, interests, purposes, financial range of grants, patterns of grant giving, deadlines, and geographic limitation. This information will help proposal writers avoid submitting improper or ineligible requests for funds. Lack of this information leads to one of the most common reasons for failure to win grants.

(e)   All contacts with funding agencies should present the proposal writer in a favorable fashion. That is, the proposal writer should be seen in a completely professional demeanor. A professional posture is seen as an asset in the eyes of the funding agency (Siegel, 1977: 43-44).

The striking importance of Siegel's study is that it supports the experience of successful grantsmen. Need more be said?

LIST OF REFERENCES

Babbie. Earl R. (1973) Survey Research Methods, Wadsworth Publishing Company, Inc.: 58.

Good, William J. and Hatt, Paul K. (1952) Methods in Social Research, McGraw-Hill Book Company, Inc.: 67-73.

Hall, Mary (1971) Developing Skills in Proposal Writing, Continuing Education Publications.

Johnson, Cheryl L. (1977) "The Effect of Creative Movement and Music as Treatment Interventions on Approach and Interactional Responses in Autistic Children," Thesis, The Ohio State University.

Krathwohl, David R. (1965) How to Prepare a Research Proposal, Syracuse University Bookstore.

McLuhan, Marshall (1967) The Meduim Is the Message, Bantam Books.

Polansky, Norman (1974) Social Work Research, The University of Chicago Press: 38-39.

Sammons, Robert L. (1975) "Goal Attainment Scaling in a Child Welfare Setting," Thesis, The Ohio State University.

Selltiz, Claire, Jahoda, Marie, Deutsch, Morton and Cook, Stuart W. (1959) Research Methods in Social Relations, Holt, Rinehart and Winston, Revised Edition: 8-9.

Siegel, June (1977) "Agency Perspectives on Factors Related to Foundations Accepting or Rejecting Grant Proposals," Thesis, The Ohio State University: 43-44.

Turabian, K. L. (1955) A Manual for Writers oe TErm Papers, Theses and Dissertations University of Chicago Press: 83-90.

Veri, Cline C. (1968) "How To Write a Proposal and Get It Funded," Adult Leadership, (March) Vol. 16, No. 9.